LEANING AGAINST TIME

SuAndi is a writer, poet and arts practitioner born and raised in Manchester. She is the recipient of an OBE, a Doctor of Arts from Manchester Metropolitan University and a Doctor of Letters degree from Lancaster University. Her awards include the Windrush Inspirational Award, Winston Churchill Fellowship, Hope & Inspiration Award for Work Supporting Black History Month, NESTA Dream Time Fellowship, Big Issue in the North Individual Inspirational Award and the MBMEN Lifetime Award. In 2023 SuAndi was the recipient, in her hometown, of the Manchester Culture Special Recognition Award. In 2024 SuAndi was named an Honorary Fellow as well as awarded the Benson Medal by the Royal Society of Literature, in recognition of 'conspicuous service to literature'.

SuAndi

LEANING AGAINST TIME

SELECTED POEMS & MARY *SEACOLE* LIBRETTO

CARCANET POETRY

First published in Great Britain in 2025 by
Carcanet
Main Library, The University of Manchester
Oxford Road, Manchester, M13 9PP
www.carcanet.co.uk

A CIP catalogue record for this book is
available from the British Library.

ISBN 978 1 80017 499 3

Book design by Andrew Latimer, Carcanet
Typesetting by LiteBook Prepress Services
Printed in Great Britain by SRP Ltd, Exeter, Devon

The publisher acknowledges financial
assistance from Arts Council England.

CONTENTS

*Some are remembered by speaking their names,
others I chose to forget. Still, they made a connection
between heart, knowledge, instinct and determination
and I will always be grateful to everyone for that.*

Whitworth Café, 17 April 2025

John McAuliffe: We've had much to and fro, SuAndi, about what to include and what to exclude for this Carcanet selection, which offers a long view of your work across the years. I wonder if you could start by telling us about the earliest poem selected here?

SuAndi: Oh heavens it would probably be 'Tantastic'.

Rochelle was the first head of the Pankhurst Centre, my best friend, and she loved going on holidays, getting a suntan. This day she had just got back from a trip and I'd gone around the desk to give her a hug when a woman came in and said to her, 'Oh, don't you look wonderful? That's an amazing colour: you're so brown!' On and on she went and I was standing there, but she never looked at me.

Then every summer, it's all about the fake tan, people talking about being golden brown – with no thought about what we Black people consider to be hypocrisy (I always use Black in the political sense with a capital B, embracing African, Caribbean and Asian heritage). Then there are those who comment about Michael Jackson, did he or didn't he bleach. I would always say: he was an amazingly talented singer, and how sad it is if he thought the only way to be really successful was to be white.

So the poem comes from that. But I had to do it in the performance in an over-exaggerated white posh voice, because once four stupid Black people asked if it happened to me… being as I am Mixed Race.

JMcA: We've talked a lot, as we worked on the manuscript, about how you have always written for performance, for the stage, a libretto, alongside pamphlets and books, and you've been anthologized for decades, but you still see performance as the frame for how you shape the work – and now you have had to think again, or reflect on, that performance element in relation to the page. And how have you thought about that over the years?

SuAndi: A performance piece is always written in my head. A poem I've written for the page I will rarely perform – I never really remember it. I might look at a performance piece and, seeing it again, notice that I don't do that line anymore, but something written for the page stays on the page. I've no idea about the mix of both kinds of poem here, no idea. Just going through the work for this collection did my head in! I found work I'd forgotten about.

JMcA: One of the interesting things for me is that there must have been 600 or 700 poems we looked at, a really big set of work that you have written over the decades.

SuAndi: And you didn't get all of them – none from the file called *Rubbish*!

JMcA: And it's a real reckoning to look back at all this work, SuAndi. What did it feel like when you were looking back on it?

SuAndi: Well, it has taken me nearly two years to deliver it to Michael [Schmidt] – and it wasn't something I was looking forward to. I think a printed record is quite scary. It's great to have done this editorial work *now*, to improve and check over work on the page. When it comes out of your mouth, it floats in the air and it's gone.

The last thing you want during a performance, is to see someone in the front row, reading along with you. You think:

put the book down. I did have somebody once say, 'you missed that line', and I said 'But it's my poem'.

JMcA: But voice carries on the page and you are a poet of voices – the book is full of other people's voices and the way you dramatize those voices, the voices of children, of working-class women, the voices of Black British people.

SuAndi: Where have the voices come from? Really, it's been about getting the audience, in particular a white audience, to see beyond me, a Black Woman. It's about the book and the cover, to get beyond that. In 'Darren', the young girl who gets pregnant, the first time I performed that, I was down south; somebody said, yes they're like that in the north. So, I had to perform that in a posher voice in the south than I did in the north. 'Nearly Forty', I do that in a Scottish accent, Liz Lochead told me it was the worst accent she'd ever heard. But it's trying to get away from just being perceived as the Black person on stage. But of course, when I want you to perceive me as a Black person on stage, I am bloody Black.

JMcA: It's an impressive *chorus* you create across the book – your poems play many parts, but they are always very interested in inequality, and very interested in weakness and in speaking *for* people, and for those other, 'unregarded' voices.

SuAndi: A lot of the poems that went into the 'rubbish' file were very early pieces when I, like every Black writer then, was writing about South Africa and the end of civil rights. With no actual life experience. Looking back, they were in some ways naive. We cannot parallel our lives in the UK, as Black people or people of African and or Asian heritage, with what happened over in South Africa and the American Civil Rights: we can't do that.

For example, when I saw that film *Unfinished Histories*, it was the last night at The Bluecoat in Liverpool. I sat on the front bench and there were probably twenty white people in the room. Right there I hated everybody in the room. I can't watch old newsreels of the Civil Rights. It hurts. The water-hose, the water cannons. I had to wait for everyone else to leave before me because I didn't know what emotion was on my face.

But it's trying to find your own voice first. Because I think almost everybody starts off writing love poems – 'Nobody loves me, nobody understands'. And then you go from there, hoping that you are developing.

JMcA: To be able to write about other people, you must know yourself. That means the poems will have that sense, that you've just talked about, of knowing the difference between who you are, in relation to the experiences you're looking at, whether they are familiar and local, or, say, international politics.

SuAndi: But it is also about having listening skills! For example there is the poem 'Just Slow'. I went to work in a school in Timperley. I couldn't find the address. It was over a little bridge, which is why I couldn't find it, and every time I stopped for directions people ran from the car pretending they couldn't hear me. Eventually I got there but late. One of the girls in the group was called Linda, she had Down's Syndrome; she spent the whole afternoon saying to me 'fookin 'ell, SuAndi, I'm stupid, but I know where school is, fookin 'ell' – what an amazing voice! She knew her limitations, but she also knew how to get across something. And I knew – 'I've got to have you'.

JMcA: And does some of this come from your time as a social worker?

SuAndi: That was later. I was in Congleton first, then I came Stockport and then I went to Whalley Range, for residential social work.

JMcA: So a lot of these voices come from those places, where you are constantly listening out.

SuAndi: I started some in Stockport but more so as I went to Manchester. I used to abscond with the kids. Lemn Sissay and I would go to do gigs, though I'd say to the staff I was going to take them to the pictures…

We had a girl in from Wythenshawe and she was stroppy, she didn't like Black people, didn't like 'coloured people' (as she said it). We went to perform in Liverpool where Lemn told his story via his poems. Over the next few days, after that, she wrote her life in poetry, her family, and it was really powerful, another voice that should be heard.

The biggest compliment is when you come across people who have carried for years one of your poems in their pocket or bag because the words mean so much to them. Wow what a compliment that is!

JMcA: The poems travel a long way from Timperley and Wythenshawe – to Australia – that 'Gordon Bennett' poem, and to North America, to Nigeria – and even as you are writing about identity and different voices, you are framing that globally.

SuAndi: Yes, that is more mature than just saying 'dead white man did that to us'. Gordon gave a talk, very early in my life in the arts, at the Tate Gallery. It blew me away and I wrote the poem and I sent it to him. And it was about two years later, he wrote back.

He said, 'No one's ever written me a poem and I didn't know how to reply'.

He was a visual artist and he kept saying, when I saw him lecture, 'I don't know why I'm here, but maybe because I am called *Gordon Bennett*'. You know that phrase, *Gordon Bennett*, and he put some work up that didn't seem very interesting. But then he put an image up – it was two trees with a woman inverted, tied at the ankles between the trees – and he said, 'that's my mother, they're checking for her virginity'. She was one of the 'Stolen Generation'.

Then he showed different work. More Aboriginal-connected. People were muttering, 'it's not supposed to be things like this in here', old intellectual vanguards of the arts. When he'd finished, I just sat there, and I remember thinking, 'Please don't hate all white people'. A woman came up and tapped me on the arm and it was his wife. I think she was white. I think they were married. We walked to the front, I just thanked him and walked away.

JMcA: That's a great story. And it reminds me too that the visual arts have been very important to you. How have they influenced you as a writer? Or do you feel your curatorial work and your work with visual art are different things?

SuAndi: My art teacher told my mother at parents' evening: 'We usually put people into the 'O' level arts for the extra one but we'll not bother with SuAndi, she can't tell the top of a painting from the bottom'. We were copying Italian Renaissance in our books. Then The Cornerhouse hosted 'The Image Employed', and suddenly I and other people and all the members of BlackScribe saw ourselves on the wall. We'd never seen ourselves on the wall. You know, huge impact, right?

Then I started to get commissions to write narrative for exhibitions. My first one was a Victorian exhibition at Manchester City Art Gallery. At the time it didn't work for me but the young people, all Black girls, they wrote. But at the time it just didn't inspire me. Seeing yourself, something you recognise, does inspire words. Definitely, going to work in the United States and seeing work in the States was for me an amazing experience in my development.

JMcA: Do you want to say something about this book's cover, a brilliant image by Faith Bebbington?

SuAndi: The work that Faith does, usually made from recycled material, basically rubbish – I just love her work. She's done probably five covers for the National Black Arts Alliance and me. In this sculpture, there's a cockiness in it that I like.

JMcA: If the international dimension comes across clearly, in the visual element too, you are also a poet of a specific place: of the city of Manchester and its people, and the structures which shape how people relate to one another in the city.

SuAndi: It's a funny thing. I said not so long ago, there is an egotistic element to a Manchester writer now – you can get an email with twenty lines on their career – in a three-line message. People are so busy banging their ego-drum. When I came into the arts, quite late in life, there was more of a collective nurturing. There were places you could meet. The Cornerhouse café, the Greenroom. You could watch other people's work. Henry Normal and I would go and see every poet that came to town, yeah, and I'd be sitting there thinking, 'People who walk up and down. Oh God, I hope I don't do that.' I remember thinking, I will sit on a chair even on the edge of the stage. And I'm definitely not going to say 'The poem speaks for itself'. Now whenever I watch a performance, I want to be made jealous by the artist. I want to be saying, 'oh my God they are so good, I need to go home and practice'. I don't want to sell anything that's just – *alright*.

JMcA: You capture that social world around performance in one of the poems here, where you're waiting outside a reading and a man starts upbraiding you…

SuAndi: That was at the Anthony Burgess Centre – and we hadn't even gone in! I don't know who he was. He just started on me. You have that, an element of racism. I live my life in the arts and people come up to me and say, 'Oh, so *you're* SuAndi'. Sadly these are all white people who have been 'warned' about me and I think 'Here we go'.

I had dinner the other night with someone, and I had to tell them why I didn't want to read someone else's poem as a voice-over. I was ready for an uncomfortable meeting, but before I had even sat down she said, 'I want to tell you I am so honoured to meet you'. Of course not all meetings with Black people go well but the majority do.

If you're outspoken and sometimes out of order, which I have been loads of times, the white gaze identifies you as 'trouble'. The Black gaze shouldn't always say, 'Oh, we support you for that'. But that can happen, as in this generation – it is so ego-based. For me NBAA has been wonderful, as I learnt so much from all the artists I worked with.

JMcA: Looking back at this body of work of yours in Manchester, how do you see the work in relation to other kinds of northern writing now, as well as that of your peers in in the rest of Britain?

SuAndi: The fact I was in BlackScribe was really important: we didn't always get on, but it was such an important starting point. And so was doing the job at Cultureword. I'd never done anything in the arts. I'd kind of written this family saga, my own family, of which I had sent off the original copy (it was all done on carbon paper) to a publisher. He sent it back, bless him, saying, 'it's quite good but not enough racism in it'.

I came at writing completely naïve; I began as an administrator. BlackScribe started and I asked if I could join them, to help with performances and watch them. Then I thought, I could do that and get paid! My very first performance, I was co-MC with Lemn *and* performing: we had the Kings and Queens of Black poets – John Agard and Grace Nichols, Jean 'Binta' Breeze... How can I forget when it came to introducing John Agard and saying, 'I'm ever so sorry, but it seems John hasn't turned up' – and he came down the stairs, performing. I was blown away. I didn't realise how young they were then. Last Saturday I had dinner with Linton Kwesi Johnson and John Cooper Clarke before their show. I'm there now as a professional equal, colleague and friend. I think the old guard recognise non-ego. I don't think established people need you to be in their face – blowing your own trumpet; saying I've done that, I've done that, I've done that.

Whenever I was in the States, Amiri Baraka would say, 'come on, girl, let's hit the hood. When he came to Manchester, Corrine Fowler was brought in to introduce him because they decided no one in Manchester was good enough to do so. I said to Corrine, just do it, but I'm coming to meet him because I know him. He was waiting at the Midland Hotel when I walked in and he said, 'what are you doing here?' I said, 'you're in Manchester, my home town'.

I think if life gives you such opportunities, be quiet and listen. Listen to people like Amiri, like Maya Angelou who

I chatted to a few times over the phone. A writer always needs to listen. You know, I listen to conversations all over the place.

JMcA: Those names are a history of a kind of British poetry. Amiri Baraka and Maya Angelou and that American world also, but I'm interested in how your work interacts with Linton Kwesi Johnson, John Agard, Grace Nichols, Lemn Sissay. Poets whose voices also come off the page.

SuAndi: Lemn and I, you know, have fallen out and then made friends so many times over the years. I have this thing with Lemn, I say 'I hate you', which means, that poem is amazing. There were periods, when we were performing together, we weren't speaking. So I'd walk past and say, 'I hate you'[laughing]. He in turn hated that. I've always said, sometimes you write work that just blows me away. It just blows me away and I have no hesitation to say that to any artist if their work is as amazing.

JMcA: But the live literature world can be a funny business. I'm sure you've been the last one on at open mike nights with the entire audience reading before you...

SuAndi: The very first Manchester Poetry Festival was organised by Henry Normal. He said to me, I've got Wendy Cope coming. Do me a favour, he said, pick her up. So, I picked her up and we went and had dinner. And she said, 'Don't you hate it when you've agreed everything and then they say, we're going to open with local poets. Who have been told ten minutes and will do ten poems (that's not ten minutes)'. So we talked about that. Then she said, 'who the bloody hell am I on with tonight, SuAndi?' And I went, 'Me'. And she says, 'You're not *local*, don't you ever let them say that. It undermines a poet.' After that I've avoided being called local again.

JMcA: Even though your poems *are* very grounded in these places, not too far from where we are sitting today.

SuAndi: You hear writers saying they write in isolation, they write every day. But I think if you're going to talk about life, then you have to listen to people around you and be aware of people, to see people. Not to be tunnel-visioned. Our role is not only to record society but also to question it. Very much in these times we have to question it, and to tell the stories that people can't tell in the way we can.

UNTITLED

I speak in English.
Think in English.
Read in English.
Live beside the English.
Survive the English.
Appear English.
But my soul is African.

I'M TIRED OF PROTESTING OUTSIDE[1]

I am tired of protesting outside
I want to be inside
Where it's warm and they are serving coffee
With odd tasting sandwiches and biscuits single wrapped
You can throw your crumbs to the birds

I have taken to the streets so many times
My feet are blistered
Can I now stand by the lectern?
With a microphone instead of my mouth
Working like a megaphone
My lungs burn from inhaling the fumes of all this shit
I'd like to breath in the air of power and exhale with reason
Tired of screaming my rights it ain't right

I have signed so many petitions my hand writes as I am sleeping
Now I click my support from one campaign to the next
And still I am outside
Ostracized
To the inside
Where you gather to talk of me
In hushes tones in case I am listening

We can't hear you at the back
While you refuse to speak louder
For fear your conspiracies will really spark a revolution

And I am armed
Part of an army of many
Across the many hues of my people
You can keep on scheming

We will weep and bury our fallen
Pushed over and stomped on by you
Generation after generation
But we see your fear
And what we cannot see we smell
Just like equality
It's in the air blowing closer and closer and closer

THE BOX

I didn't keep it there in the beginning.
In the beginning I put it on a shelf.
It was nothing in size shape dimensions
Like anything I had imagined.
But to be honest, my imagination
Hadn't spent anytime anticipating its arrival.
So the truth is a lot of time had passed before I found the courage
To bring it home.
And then with no plans,
I put it on the shelf.
And that is where it stayed
Until an unexpected guest sent me scurrying
To freshen the spare room.
How could I explain
A heavy white cake box,
I couldn't.
So just for one night
(I thought).
I pushed it under the bed
To keep company with shoes lost
Some single without a partner,
And where dust without the energy to roll
Lay like mini blankets of grey
Holding the box safe.
A protection from the heaviest of mattress rolls.
I never took it out.
Never checked on its condition.
But I never forgot it was there.
Moving from bed to bath
Up and down the stairs
The white cake box

Hit my senses
Like a spirit on the landing.

When Africa beckoned my return
Going home
Seemed close enough a home
To take home
So down I went
My knees marked by the tufts of the carpet.
My arms stretched far
Until I pulled it close to me
Stood, the box cold next to my chest,
My heart.
Then before I locked my luggage
I carefully placed it secure under the zipper
In Ghana I walked a beach
Of pure white sand damp with the lapping blue
Holding the box for the last time
As I walked into the waves
Letting the contents fall
And left my father in the sea

PICTURE

someone painted a picture of herself
but it had no face. it wasn't a painting but a photograph

of one arm suspended by nothing
held up by emptiness

in it there were many colours
all neutral

it was a black and white the scenery was vast.
And she had painted every detail
in wide white sweeps
the arm was a negative
so dark I could make out every pore of flesh
she called it 'me'
and I recognised myself.

STRONG BLACKWOMEN

Strong Blackwomen work
day time night time long time
do not sleep
but bypass exhausted from foot to bed replacing
desktop worktop for pillows to lay their heads
Strong Blackwomen do not dream but rework needs
rotas agendas itineraries and never therefore
try to check the space behind them
dawn brings thoughts to mind of the day ahead
this day like all days is a work day
they stretch their legs lay hands across strong thighs
and allow only a microsecond thought for the space behind them
Strong Blackwomen shower clean
exercise lotion and beautify to hold
themselves against the wrath of the day
they have no time to think of the space behind them
Strong Blackwomen stretch their lips
to smile to speak to get the message across
and wrap taut fingers round long tobacco stems
to kiss themselves into a sense of contentment
to escape the thought of that space behind them

LAST NIGHT I WENT TO LISTEN TO POETRY

I did not recognise the face that called my name
It is not unusual there are so many white people
And alas so many are forgettable
Unless their spirits shine as my many friends do
Or glow menacingly in enemy hue
I accept the invitation to sit
And prattle a friendly chat
Trying to locate a connection
The man tells me he recognised my profile
I jest because of the large fatness of my cheeks
The man asks if my wig was expensive

The man remarks on my absence from the arts
I update with no embarrassment
Arts Council axing, house sale
and a move to rental
The location surprises his Didsbury abode
And I move on a topic

The man mentions his stroke it visible on his body
And I speak of mine
Much smaller but to ease any awkwardness
I knew the man said that you waved the Black banner
Now you can use disability too
Are you also lesbian?

The poet we are waiting on greets me
Might have known you would know him the man said
The poet is Black.
Together we go to collect our tickets
I have pre-ordered

Not as the man suggests
Blagged a freebie.

The host lays out the evening
After the writers speak they will take questions from the floor
Don't you start a heckle
The man whispers

The writers talk of travel
The places they love
Where they live
Elif Shafak speaks of London
A cosmopolitan haven
In which she feels save
She wouldn't say that of Sharston
The man spits in my ear
I raise my hand to block and bar him from me
I shake in my seat
Kei Miller stares at me wondering what is wrong
When the evening is over
The man leans and asks
Did you enjoy that?
My silence is the only thing the man hears

THE HOUSE STOPPED BREATHING, – ALMOST

The house stopped breathing, – almost
The daily inhale, exhale stopped – almost
Windows basked in sunlight failed to open
So cool breezes could not tickle away the dewdrops of a morning's
    expectation
As doors opened to find no one waiting there
And dust lingered hopefully for a tender hand to wipe it into order
Winters became simply dark
As drawn curtains no longer embraced to keep it warm
So the house stopped breathing – almost

Night workers took detours
And drunks hallucinated passed
As the house would sometimes shudder
Trying to re-establish its foundations
And the old chimney, many years without purpose
Would burp out a puff of sadness
And it seemed as though the trees would choir
A protective sigh the leaves shivering together

After a few years
There was hustle and bustle
As old suitcases and packing boxes
Scattered themselves across the floors
Until stacked carefully
Left the rooms as empty as a discarded soul
And the house's breathing became so shallow
It felt sure it had stopped – almost

Then one morning voices of excitement
Waited expectedly in the garden

Waking the house with a curiosity
And when it saw so many gathered
And in their midst the face of a mother
It took in air with such sharpness
That every window opened wide in excitement
For the house knew, she had not returned
But it had a duty once again
To shelter a family
And the house began to breathe deeply

It takes time to fund a revolution
And practice
And our lives have been in full dress rehearsal
Since long time.
Revolutions don't evolve but erupt.
Sometimes with planning
Other times not.
Man's spark blows easy.
Bud in one hand, weed other.
Yet still armed enough to kill,
Split a bitch's lip,
Hurt a friend
Rape a lover 'til dead

This revolution has no heroes.
They be simply wars
I'm planning something larger,
Well large,
National, international, global.
I'm in negotiation with the skies
Speaking to family on another planet.
Serious tactics with Sirius B.

My revolution is going to blow out
The final frontier
Women going forward
Man aside,
This side and this side
No petty gender squabble
This be one huge Black 'Motherfucker' of a revolution
And when it done
The Blues will be a white thing.

It sits comfortable on dusty shelves
In dark rooms dank in smell
And holds its breath for one who comes
To turn its leaves of fantasy
And believe that every one reveals a truth
A branch reaching back to yesterday

It knows its place
In well-lit designed libraries
Where students comply and do not question
Just copy and rework for the essays
Their futures depend on
While the public run their fingers
Across titles seeking biographies
Celebrities whose history might
Last a year maybe more probably less

History knows it's best
To say little of truth
Not confess a lie
But in detail claim
That's how life was then.
A defence that takes no responsibility
For today's bigotry
The blanket of lies falsehoods
Knitted into the camouflage of truth
History knows its place

TOAST

She offered me toast with my tea
Not cake or biscuits
Maybe because of the hour of the day
Brewed the right way
Like my mother's teapot
warmed first
Old ways seem odd today
Toast in three minutes
always golden
No aroma
to tempt the appetite
Cookers with grills
foil wrapped to save bacon fat
No bending backache with eyelevel vision
central heating modernised away what once was to no longer
It's not the same
as when
One fork too heavy for the table
slightly bent by the heat
of a grate red hot with coals
browned fingers
often burnt toast
It made no difference
when laden with fridge rock hard butter
Smells of the old are different to the new
I sipped my tea and declined the marmalade

ORDINARY WOMAN

I am an ordinary woman
Nothing special
Ordinary. Nothing. Nothing. Ordinary.
There is nothing to show
Nothing to tell
Ordinary. Nothing. Ordinary.
I have cut my hair, grown it
Cut it again. Permed it, straightened it, left it natural
Ordinary. Natural. Naturally ordinary.

I have raised children, alone
Born many, lost a few
Terminated one for my survival, sanity.
Paid the price. Murderer. Nothing. Ordinary.

Will you tell of me?
Remember me in history?
I am not a feminist made no stands
Nor have I been the discarded
Pleasure of a man.
I have loved and left. Loved and lost.
Ordinary. No different. Ordinary.

Yet without me there is no tomorrow:
No more generations;
Without me the world cannot last
From my loins – I have borne life,
Ordinary children
Grinded by a man, ordinary just like me.

Do not forget we who have fought battles
Lost and won wars
Worked hard in labour
Settled no scores;
You may go down in history,
We will simply die.
Ordinary. Nothing.
Ordinary in life. Ordinary in death. Ordinarily special.
This woman me, that man he
Please, never forget the ordinary people.

THE WIG

When the Chemo started –
courtesy of the National Health –
each woman was given a replacement
for her loss

My mother, Clairol-assisted by
'Nice 'n' Easy' over the years
weakened now by the ravages of radium
propped herself up and waited
and could not believe her ears when told –
lucky lady, still glossy and almost a full head –
that she wouldn't need hers

Bugger off! she said
finding a power we all thought had
dissipated through treatment

Did you think I've scrubbed floors
raised two kids
worked every hour God sends
laboured at overtime
and never once drawn Benefit
that I am going lie here
and be cheated out of what is by rights mine?

Then reached out to grab from the trolley
the closest one to hand, not caring one hoot
for its style, length or colour, shoving it almost
with the truculence of a child under her pillow
where I retrieved it and brought home
as testament to her life.

SOPHIA ALLWEISS[4]

Sophia Allweiss got vexed one day
And took that flag
And wrapped it bandana red around her brunette tresses
Pulled out her pistol
And went looking to shoot herself a man

Thought she saw danger
In the whites of his eyes
The power of murder in his hands
The demon of lust in his thighs
And all her nightmares
Between Hebrew heaven and hell
Here and there
In the deep shadows of his skin

Years later
With her grans playing at her feet
Fed from the toil of her labour
Cooking baked with love
She would tell a story
Wrapping her Montana twang around the Yiddish
About the day
She tried to push back the sea
And change the tide
And found herself lacking
Found instead the core
Of her humanity and love

KEEPS ON GROWING

She was amazed.
No one noticed
Could see it
She felt sure there was
A deep indentation in her jumper
The light fabric of her favourite dress
Which, if she was honest with herself
She no longer had the strength to wear
She had considered going to her doctor
But a chance meeting in the supermarket
Had only achieved a debate
NHS cuts and the waiting time for beds
These days her bed was an alien planet she feared
So many long hours awake
Found her sleeping on the settee
Time does not heal
It simply expands what is
Into what can never be
Just like the hole in her heart
Since he left
It simply kept on growing

POWER

I search for women
women I search for them
In positions of authority equality
Power is a man's game
I check panels at meetings
speakers, presenters
searching for women
Days when I am complaining in places
other then Marks & Sparks
I search for women
As bank managers, tax officers, heads of departments, gynaecologists
Some days I spy one and I smile smugly claiming this woman as me
We have progress all is not defeat
There are women out there
And when I do locate
I back track just to see how many of them were Black

ABASINDI MAWGA WOMEN[5]

Mawga women
Strike poses in 6, 8, 10; sizes
Of sharp angled hips
Stomachs iron-flat
And breast-less silhouettes
In clothed enviable perfection

But nakedness reveals
Knee bones protruding
Thighs, calves, forearms twinning
And arses hard to recognise.

These are the models
That sashay across our vision
As we purse our lips
In dismay disgust dejection

While our hands caress
The rise of belly
That folds into an apron of warm flesh

When we bend our breasts lead
Identical dancers in motion
The dimples of our elbows are deep
Our knees are satin cushions
Our lips cheek full
And when we turn to leave
Our hips are pivoting sensuality

We are not stereotype caricatures of Africa
Mawga women
Come in shades
Black and white
As do we

ONCE

Once I was 8
Satin red ribbon wrapped ringlets
Growing into a right madam
With enough sass for twice my age
Once I was eight

Once I was 13
Flaring spots
Puppy fat weeping
No one understood me
A true teenage demon
Once I was 13

Once I was 24
Slim slender sleek
Femininity my art of war
Men were so meek
When I was 24

Once I was 33
All my future ahead
Every door a door of opportunity
Independent,
Relying only on me
Once I was 33
When did I become 40?

Once I was 40
Still dreaming
Of breast feeding
Morning coffee mothers' meetings

School gate waiting
Homework helping
Her first lipstick
Her first kiss
Mother of the Bride weeping
Do people still knit?
I will
Helping and remembering how nappy changing
Biological clock ticking
Ticking ticking
41 43 44 and more and more and

Once I was
Don't say the number
Smile when age is spoken
Let a joke drop
And laugh
But never tell never never never
Puppy grew into maturity
Little girl let loose and flew
If only you had known me when I was young

SHIRLEY

When I was a child
My mother wanted me to grow up to be
Another Shirley Bassey.
Gold Finger
He's the man, the man with the Midas touch.[6]

Why Shirley?
Because she had made it.
She had gotten out.
And we loved her.
The glamour, those painted nails
and THE DRESSES!
Cut low at the back and low at the front.
Even the wigs.
We all thought we had problems with our hair then.

Trouble was, all my friends' mothers
Wanted them to be another Shirley too.
You think that's funny?
It's not, it's sad.

Oh, we knew about people over in America
But Shirley was one of us.
She was our only Shero. Because our past
had been locked away by the key of His-tory.

Now I'm grown
I have discovered that there are hundreds,
Thousands of people in my ancestry
For me to be proud of
Great scholars, inventors, historians, discoverers.

So now, when my children grow up,
They will have many examples to aspire to
And every reason to be Black and proud.
For me will never again allow Black achievement
To be locked away by the key of His-tory.
European history.
And we'll not forget Shirley
She will have her place in the Black Book of Fame.
Who could forget Shirley?
Hey, Big Spender, spend a little time with me.[7]

Did you hear that creak that wasn't there last week.
The Doc will say it's a phase but I know it's old age.
Come on take a guess, I don't mind I'll confess –
I'm nearly 40.

I was in a shop the other day,
You should have seen this girl's outfit –
It was disgusting – she had everything on display,
But in a colour that really goes with the shade of my hair.
And I thought dare I? Yes I dare!
So I asked the assistant for a size ------'teen.
And you should have heard what she said to me,
You know I could have scream.
But I told her,
Of that have no doubt –
Lady like, I didn't shout,
Well not really.

I said that fashion had style and class in my day,
And if I had a flippin' daughter
I'd never allow her to dress that way.
And the prices, they have got a cheek –
I mean do they really think I was born last week...
I mean, I'm nearly 40.

But my figure's good,
Ok it's generous, but proportioned –
But God I do look rough in the morning –
But Sheila from Brookside, she was no awning –[8]
And she was married twice and must have been all of 46
And I'm only nearly 40, me.

And I'm fit I make sure of it.
To check against arthritis I've started using a menthol rub.
The other morning it fell down side of tub.
I thought I'm not risking a dislocated hip,
Anyway who gives a sh–
I'll take up aerobics.
Or keep fit,
Yoga possibly.
I mean you can't get too strenuous at 40.

As for the menopause,
If it means an end to periods –
I'll welcome it with applauds
What's a little hot flush,
Just a mere rush of blood
But the cold sweats,
Christ what a mess
I feel like 50.

And some days I'm really depressed,
And I seem to need a lot more rest,
And I really am loath to confess
That if some bloke offered me a jump –
I'd have to walk it.

But in lots of ways,
I've had some fabulous days.
I mean you could be flat on your back –
And from my experiences –
There's absolutely no pleasure in that
To tell you the truth I don't miss my youth
I'm looking forward to being 40.

THE STIRRUP TEST

Seems to me that this man
Has the coldest hands in creation,
And eyes so small –
No wonder they demand close vision.
Turning my head
So my chin is propped on my chest,
I notice how his eyebrows would flatter
A toupee.
Either that or my pubes have been
Growing with abandonment
Since the last time I had a look down there.

Chatting with your dentist
With your mouth full of steel
Is one thing –
But see here,
With my legs hoisted on stirrups,
It's hardly the time for a tete-a-tete.

You've a lovely pair of ovaries, he says
Well I have to admit,
That's my first compliment
In that particular department.
Have I, I said.
Oh yes,
And as productive as a woman in her thirties.
Well good for me,
Seeing as I am exactly
Six months, four days and seven and a half hours away
From forty.
I suppose that's a compliment too.

He continues.
I'll just take a sample swab
You won't feel much more then a small prick
Well I've been here before -
More times than I care to recall.

It's the way they scrub their hands that gets me.
You'd think them rubber gloves
Were a figment of the imagination.
All the time smiling,
And you with your arse still directed
At an open door.

You can pop your pants on now, he says
And you can pop yours off, dear Doctor,
And I'll show you
What gynaecology is really about.
Sweet Mother of Jesus maybe you did have the right idea.

So how old did you say you were again?
Again, I tell him,
This time omitting the half
As I smell the whiff of sympathy.

And you're still active?
Active –
What does he think I am? –
Geriatric.
Well I'm hardly jumping off wardrobes
But when I'm really adventurous
My settee has been a forum for lust.
Well one time, that is.

Odd, very odd, he says.
And your mother ?
Dead, I say.
Dead because by the time
You decided to cut her open
She had rotted –
But I say nothing,
Just sit there looking
Whilst he turns the volumes
Of my medical history –
The war and peace of female disorder.

Well Miss, er Miss...
He's forgotten my name,
And we've been dating
Via appointment for the last year.
We could be wrong
Yes, I think
But you're positive –
It would appear your life's over –
Pity you didn't consider
Settling down,
Putting your career on hold.
I mean you can still have an active sex life,
But you'll never be a mother.
You've missed the boat, so to speak,
In fact it's sinking.
Your life's blood has ebbed away -
Stopped –
Period.

Strange how I,
Prepared for the worst,
Realise I am suddenly embarrassed
As I feel the first throes of a hot flush coming on.

I REMEMBER

I remember a fridge
As big as a place
And a front room that sparkled
With cups and medallions
For boxing and dancing and roller skating

I remember the sound of laughter
Sisters united in blood
Separated by income
One of them cleaning
The other preening

I remember hair that glowed red like sunset
And a voice unheard in company
But loud with stories with family

I remember the disbelief
And our pride
That you were the eldest
And I thought you taller
Then the Eiffel tower
And just as old

I remember the trips
The surprise transportation
From home to home
In all the cars you never owned

I remember growing
Growing up growing away
And missing you

SHE TELLING SECRETS[9]

She telling secrets.
Secrets
Who told you is right
To wash dirty clothes outside
Full view of people
Not of your blood, your skin, your colour.

No one tell you
Smut feeds hungry minds eager for scandal
Fingers extending in accusation
That we no good
Never have been
Never will.

Better tell Anansi fact and fiction
Relating relations
Right to the root of Mother Africa
With all her branches extended full of leaves
And those leaves are we

Better tell history
Of great, great, great long time grand ancestor
Sold and cargoed
Whipped and raped till black as cherry
Birth itself in smooth brown
Tell this story
So they can never forget
How far we come
How far we travel
How great our endurance

Don't tell about ghetto style breeding
Laying down with any
Skirt raised high
And leaving too many faces with the same
Tooth gap and droop eye
And Prince Charlie humongous ears

Tell about the church
A belief in the Trinity
'Rice and Peas' keeping warm
Or fou-fou ready in the pot

Tell about white gloves
White hat
And shoes...
Lord have mercy how me feet a fire
And elegant men in small trilby
And knife sharp creases
Descending to mirror glaze shine of leather

Don't foul the air
With strange women in khaki jeans
Arm muscle solid
Reaching out publicly to bring close
Another just like herself

Don't tell about sweet looking men
Sweet smelling
Sweet talking
With not one word of interest in any Sistah
Just infecting us all with his nastiness
So now even love risks infection

Gal me know you no stupid
See you uniformed to school
Cheeky to college
So why you never learn
No speak our business in public
White people be listening
And best we tell them nothing

A SLUT'S WARNING

Always keep your hands clean,
And when they're dirty don't touch your clothes.
Use a hankie to blow your nose –
Or else you'll end up with sticky cuffs,
And an upper chin dry with nasty stuff.

And your shoes should always shine,
Keep your legs crossed all the time,
Else I'll deny you're a daughter of mine –
Sluts are easy to identify.

Accidents are a fact of fate,
Prepare now later is too late;
For nurses will gossip at a rapid rate
If your underwear bears yesterday's date.

So daily change your underwear,
Check if any holes are there;
And when you toilet make sure your skirt's flat,
Always run a hand down your back –
Sluts are quick to show
What decent folk don't want to know.

Wear gloves when you go to church,
Walk with straight back-ogres lurch.
Stand close whilst I teach you a curse
To keep the devil at bay.

Vinegar keeps windows shining bright.
Dirty curtains are neighbour's delight,
And draw them before you put on the light –
Unless you intend charging.

Too much salt kills a man's prowess.
Bolt your doors and windows before you rest,
Unless you wish to invite
A no good fly-by lover.

Hot irons will turn spit to sizzle.
Ladies don't bray they giggle;
And only sluts walk with a wiggle –
I see you learnt that quickly.

Never smile at men you don't want to know.
Remember every husband has his own home,
But set your traps now before you're old –
Sluts and spinster get lonely.

Check out the man who is checking you –
Don't waste tears on a lover that doesn't love you;
And when love burns out don't sing the Blues –
Only fools marry for love.

Don't get fat before your wedding day.
Only give a little, don't go all the way.
Some slut will know if he has a problem that way –
Remember therapy costs money.

To you I give all my wisdom:
These are the secret skills of women.
I assume you don't intend living on your back –
Daughter, you surprise me

SHE NEVER SAW HER FATHER

She never saw her father young,
Flirtatious.
Entrancing her mother with stories
From under African skies

Impossible of her to imagine
The wondrous expressions of strangers
When he strode in white cloth flowing
And traditional dashiki
Or regular in C&A off the rail[10]
Bri Nylon aspiring suit of suitability

By the time she was wise enough
To miss him,
He had gone.

Over the days, weeks, months, years of living
She tried to visualise the absent half
Of her identity
Wondering where he had left his mark

Stroking her jaw line
Tracing an eyebrow
Or in her love of words
Her talent for telling stories

But he had gone
Before she could feast on him
Savour his fullness
Fill the space beneath her heart

With that peculiar scent of fatherhood
He had gone

The migrant had migrated
Left home
To go home
Turned his back on family
Because his family needed him now
Left his child
For his children
Dumped the dark brown suit of acceptability
To be robed as a man in the cloth of his people

FERNANDO[11]

After he left me
It became my habit
To watch, observe, and learn
Sides of him
That he did not realise he exposed

After he left
Animated conversations
Were communicated
By the chewing movement of his jaw
For my lip reading
His doctrines on manhood

Standing I became to realise
How small he was
Sitting
How fragile.
Strange that until he left me
This man was all the man
I had aspired to grow into

When he left
There was no major upheaval
No belongings packed
No taxi hailed
Waiting wheels displacing earth
His chariot of fire

There were no waves of farewell
Just a flying fist
The extension of his body

Signifying fury
Striking virgin skin
Freshly razored and exposed

That I the youth
The son of his loins
Should have the audacity
To think myself man enough
Independent enough
To draw a blade
Without blood letting
Without his permission
Was sufficient to stop him still
Before he turned and left me
Fatherless

Times change
Soap, steel and water
Are now electronic aluminium precision
Of closer then the closest shave
And when I stand
Face to face with myself
Reflected in the mirror of all seeing
How strange it is to me
To see my father there
After all these years
Since I left him

YOU HAVE AFRICAN CALVES[12]

You have African calves
(Though your shoes would anger my father)
Still I remember
The shine of skin
Revealed between sock and trouser cuff
And remember
How I would stare in wonder
That legs so thin
Could carry my father.

I feared sometimes
When he, my uncle
And other men gathered
I making up for an absent son
And would sit at his feet
In silence.
Enjoying the music of their speech
And hold my breathe
To stop a laughter (flow)
Of so many thin sticks
A ridicule of interruption
Of their debating
Like politicians
Totally earnest
In their passion
Talking the fullness of nothingness
But ennobling the ancestors
By this simple coming together

You have African calves
Lined up upon African ankles

Fragile yet strengthen by history
To carry you
Across barriers
Over hurdles
Tidal waves of resistance
Where I laughed as a child
I now sit in wonder
At their might

SOUTHERN

Sweat wrapped him in a muskiness
that would have been sexy on a frame
thirty years younger
25 pounds heavier, firmer
now it suggested stillness
like mothballs
on a suit worn only for funerals
occasionally a tear had the nerve
to free itself and begin a slow flow down his nose
then it would linger at the corner of his mouth
a vain attempt to moisten
lips cracked and bleeding
but he didn't weep
old yellow eyes seeming dead
concentrated on the way forward
looking down they saw only dirt
and they knew dirt in all its disguises
speeding up
his body moved easily
through a neighbourhood of no-importance
to him – this day – people
and when he reached her
his large hands southern
reached out with a tenderness
of a father who loves the touch of his daughter

INTERGENERATIONAL TRAUMA

My father first walked the earth in Warri
His feet sinking into the hot mud of Nigeria's Delta State
Then one day, as other men launched fishing boats
He sailed far away.
Why, I don't know,
He never told me,
I never asked.
Africa and Manchester did not offer life parallels
So we never had that conversation

My father never talked of the past
I never asked
What did you do in the war dad?
What was your home like?
Do I look like your people?
Can you see your mother in my eyes?
The way I walk, argue
I'm built a female version of you
Am I the same height as your father?
Words never spoken
Only got silent responses.

My father never said
When the white man came:
But I know he knew.
Summers we would visit his old master
Exchanging our terrace house
For a large white detached in Richmond Surrey
Where my father cleaned;
A servitude repayment for our visit.
While I was forbidden to

Touch, speak, play,
Do anything without first asking permission.
Strange white people I thought.
'Snobby bastards,' said my mother when I returned home
'Where do they think this is?
It's not bloody Africa.'
Her temper causing her cheeks to flame red
Matching the copper of her hair
'Andi,' she'd say
'Slavery is over;
Get over it.'
What did she mean?
But I never asked
And she never explained.

Schools for my father
Were glorious European opportunities
So he spared nothing to buy
My uniform, my shoes
A too large briefcase.
Copies of the same books that teachers
Distributed daily in class.
Strange, that I had to leave the classroom
To begin my education;
Tutored via overheard conversations
Documentaries, radical articles
And orators from Marcus Garvey to Malcolm X.
Even though neither had a liking for white people.
But no matter how I broadened my knowledge,
I still loved my mother
Nothing was going to change that.
Now my mouth was full
Of words my brain had memorised
Colonialism, lynchings, detention

Apartheid, segregation
Civil Rights, Black Power
And always
Slavery.

What did my father know?
That the Yorubas were favoured for their strength
But whipped long to curb their independence
That the Ibos though stolen in their thousands
Also found an inner power to walk-on water
And the ijaw from Warri
Who speaks of them?
Not, certainly, my father.
Except sometimes,
When the silence was so loud my ears would ache
I would turn to him
And he looking far into the distance
Seemed oblivious to the tears
Washing his cheeks
Flowing under his chin
Then water falling towards his heart.

In that moment my father
Was no longer the man I knew
The man I didn't know.
He was in that moment,
A body filled with the spirits of all his ancestors.
My family from my grandfather
To generations who never imagined life beyond the Forçados River
Conquered, shackled, bartered
Sold, abused, demonised, throttled, burnt, flogged
Criminalised, imprisoned,
Executed by the law under the law.

The trauma of the new
The wicked the evil
Filled my father
So that he could not speak
And I never asked why.
Why,
Before he died
Was he called Thomas

Under my right eye
I have an indentation
It is in the exact same place
As my father's peoples' ritual scarring
Some days when I look at it
It seems more prominent
Like it really is a scar
But I can barely make it out
Through my tears

RITUALS

Strange that we don't have rituals
That came from back home
A place we never visited
To this place we have never left
Something that made a connection
With people we resemble
People we never met

Lost in time
Washed away by tides lapping against shores
So far apart it is difficult to imagine life
Living and lost
Are always sad moments

Nothing morbid
No shrieking or weeping
It is not sophistication that refuses to wail
More something lost in time

UNBORN

As you grew / we grew
All our thoughts / were thoughts of you
And we cared not how many knew
That our greatest need / was our need for you,

Your moods / were our moods,
Your smallest move increased our joy for you,
Our empty arms longed to hold you
To fulfil the need / we felt for you,

When you died / our hearts cried
From a wound down deep inside
And though we live on / we'll never lose
The love we planned for you.

NANDOS[13]

I wonder where you are as we gossip
The usual things family,
Men!
Men are so stupid
A waste of space
Not one of you made a good choice
She will be different
But she pays the prices
Dates are rare,
So rare
I know each one
No details
Just the excitement of expectation
I wonder if you are jealous
I suppose so
Sure
Definitely
She misses you just like me
More than I, off course
She looks so much like you
That every time she smiles
My heart cries
Then like you
She says something stupid
'Mum had such lesbian taste'
And I laugh so much I cry for real

THAT'S PART OF BEING OLD

The remembering
And fashioning it
Like a movie director
Altering characters
Making them more interesting

So, a tale becomes a fable
A historical
Fact
To pass down to children
So, when you're gone
You will be the lead player
The heroine, hero
In a time now of yesterday

That's part of being old
Manipulating
A respect
Based on longevity
Grey hair gives status
Often never achieved in youth
The 20 30 40 50
60 with new hips
New teeth 70 walking stick
Distracted at 80
Overhead conversing with the past
The ghosts of yesterday.

STRANGE

Strange
how their presence
still undermines that which we cling to so fiercely
I am my own person
so that we mark
everything
by their disapproval
and the thought of disdain
can still make a lip quiver like a three-year-old
with a tremor
remembered
from early days
Their approval
hovers over everything
cooking cleaning washing dressing
and it is true that colour never did suit
they knew
their small habits
repeated daily so that they became gigantic irritations
now
seem part of our personalities
and we find ourselves
mirroring
all that used to annoy
disregarding how different
we are
somehow
they continue to exist within us
demanding
and finding
a place in our daily lives

and no matter how singular our features of
height stature shape walk talk
somehow
they put the words on our lips
and we hear ourselves saying
the same things
in the same tones of yesterday
Mothers
they never ever let go

since you left life has gone on normal as before though not the same naturally the difference being the absence of you and i have to resist nudging you to certain tv shows and picking up your favourite angel delight whip which was always difficult as chocolate butterscotch banana strawberry and all flavours were favoured by you i know people who know me well knew me with you knew you have worried over me and found themselves congratulating even celebratory of my ability to get on with my life occasionally either brave or unthinking someone has asked do you still miss him and i smile to ease their concern and say yes naturally yes i miss his your smile endless chatter know all opinion i do not miss i miss your lips the smack of your kisses your crazy ways yes even your crazy ways but like i say since you been gone the days have passed as before and i sleep as well as ever only now with my feet on the floor whilst i lie in my bed fear i suppose that you mum dad might pull me over there with you and though i miss you all i'm not ready yet and sleep is the time when my strength is weakened and so i need to keep my feet firmly on the ground

THE SANDWICH[14]

She plans her wardrobe
Conscientiously
Nothing too short or low cut
Jewellery to decorate
Not flash as in vulgarity

The night before was always most difficult
Memories flooded
None more powerful than her own
Mother and father

She recalls one friend
And finds herself laughing
Not a wild cackle of madness
But a sound full of warmth in its release

Her thoughts run
Like a video on replay
And she finds it impossible to do
All the things she needs to do
For the normality of her day

Part of her enjoys the ritual
An opportunity to meet and greet old friends
To feel the warmth of a family
Extended into a community holding hands
Linking the past to the present
Ancestors watching rituals

Trepidation lay only in timing
Not the cynicism of

Black people are always late
But the eulogies, tears hymns, prayers
And always the preaching

She thinks
If I hear 'Amazing Grace' one more time
I will die!
Still she sings
Though sometimes she mimes the odd verse with a purpose
A signifier of a too long farewell
No disparagement to the tearful grief of sadness
Simply meeting the need of her belly
She always arrives prepared
The four-quarter substances
Of a corned beef sandwich
Which she swallows invisibly
With every Amen

ON THIS DAY OF ALL THINGS NORMAL[15]

If I said, the sun was beaming, scorching. I'd be lying
This after all is England
No, the sun was doing the best she could
And the sun is determined.
Even on the greyest day she will suddenly surge forward
Dispersing clouds
At other times, teasingly, she'll pop in and out of the showers
Laying herself lovingly across the shoulders of commuters
Scurrying along the wet streets.

Yes, over here,
The sun is not how many remember her, – Back there
But still, under her rays grass grows
Wheat waves its crown the crops harvest
Flowers bloom and trees dress themselves alive in greenery

I was watching one tree. This day, late in the year
Much the same way I have watched it all of our lives.
Sometimes my eyes discover new branches that have pushed
    their way
Past all the elders.
Stretching themselves out towards the warmth of the sun.

On this day of all things normal,
As the sun blocked my focus with her fullness.
From somewhere deep inside the earth
Air gathered into a gust of energy
And I am sure the tree moved.
And as the sun turned her face away
One single leaf, lost its grip,
Fluttered

And found itself
Falling through a tunnel of air.

The lower boughs spread to save it.
And other leaves rustled together with love trying to make a
    canopy of safety
But it was too late.
The leaf fell
And lay motionless, ghostly still
And I felt the ground beneath me groaned in its sorrow
And that cry wrapped its angst between the roots
And in the same moment of a microsecond
As she passed away
The sun back there, back home stopped shining.

DIS WOMAN[16]

Yuh know dis woman?
Yes man, mi know her,
Yuh suhre?
Yes man, mi suhre.
Yuh identify?
Yes mi identify.
Den tel mi how yuh know
Wen time past lawng
And many rivers flow
Between dis land and Babylon –
Dat dis Black mamma is youh mammy?

Because mi smell her Sah.
Smell her here in de curve of mi palm,
Where she lead mi through life,
Here in the soft flesh of mi ear;
Where she whispered stories of Ashanti
Here in de small of mi back;
Where she rubbed away de terror of yout
And here in mi heart where she rested,
For all the days we separated –
Yes man mi know her.

I AM, YOUR FAMILY

I am, your family
Which wasn't the truth
Or a lie, either.
My father her husband
Lived outside our days
Leaving by his own choosing.
We, mother and daughter,
Were so different, yet similar.

No one questioned my father
But my mother fought for recognition
At parents' evenings
Hospital appointments
Everywhere we went
Together

I am your family
She told me; cursing the air she breathed
Every time I risked my life
In the foolishness of late nights out
Too close canoodling with boys too young
To make their own families

Saturday nights, her one day of leisure
I would watch my mother
And worry that the swell of her breasts
And fullness of stomach
Might pass gene to gene to my slim form
I looked close and slightly disapproving
Of the pale alabaster of her skin
Compared to the rich nutty brown of my own

Now she is gone, left for ever
I find her in habits and rituals
I remember were hers, now mine.
Now alone I understand
I was loved totally by my mother
She was all my family

HANDS

My mother bleached
Kitchen tops
Toilet bowls
Curtain nets, bed sheets,
That dazzled white
against the redness of her hands
Now I handle life in different shades
Of polished hues manicured nails
And thank my mother for all she did
To make a lady of her daughter

THAT BLACK LAD

Her hopes were not pipe dreams
Childhood and the church had seen to that
In the ways of the Lord
Making do was a virtue
Three hail Marys to that
And she was realistic
She knew prejudice would always
Be present
Full of pre-assumptions all of them
Wrong vile bigotry
She saw it often on the way to school
Parents evening
The Christmas play ignoring the whisperings
They did not realise it was she that the words hurt
Good looks advantage for many
Made fathers fear for their daughters
While mothers had lustful dreams of possibilities that were impossible
So bad behaviour of the smallest error she berated like a demon
    demented
Time and time again
She held his head in her hand
The other across her breasts
As she repeatedly her mantra
All I want for you my son
Is to prove them wrong
Get a job
One I can be proud of
So when I go to the shops and say
That Black lad is mine

LIKE MY MOTHER

Old ladies tell me I look like my mother
And I can see her perfectly
For I paid the price of love to have her etched into my heart
When I think of who I resemble,
I see my father's hand
The fingers are bent
Permanently
The cruelty of being a prisoner of war
The skin is shiny, taunt, like deep brown leather
It is moving towards me
To trace the line of my eye
Then a gentle descent down my cheek
He is looking for any sign that my stroke,
Bell's Palsy is still obvious
At my mouth, he pulls tenderly so my lips begin to open
When he finds nothing he smiles
I smile back
My father leans forward and kisses my cheek
And see my face reflected in perfect Nigerian symmetry
Funny that
Because old ladies tell me, I look just like my mother.

THE TWIN

My mother had one
just the same

Not identical
naturally
thankfully

It wasn't that I hated it
but with the disdain of a teenager
I wanted it to be hidden
under wraps
constrained in public
whereas my mother favoured hers
with an affection of rubbing
and cooing in delight

Pampering Christmas-gifted talcum
the indulgence of cream cakes
and Bavarian slices
not to mention any-night fancied
Friday's fish and chip suppers

New Year barely passed before
Cadbury Cream Eggs supplanted
Duncan Walnut Whips

Click – click[17]

Whereas I
her daughter
have endured, sacrificed
and denied
so many temptations

And in spite – yes! –
in spite of all my efforts
the bulge that rests arrogantly
beneath my breasts
is twinned in shape and form
to the stomach-bulge belly
of my mother's.

SINGING SINATRA[18]

It makes no sense she thinks.
In this place, this time, this city
Where age has no relevance to memory
We do not forget, we are not allowed to,
We do not want to:
Staunch is entrenched in the genes of ritual.
Where there is no harm in a quick tipple on the way to mass
Or an afternoon at the bar
To debate in length the morning's preaching.

In this place so many names seem engraved
In the mouths of grandparents
Who repeat them incessantly to make sure
Those listening understand.
Lullabies and Once Upon a Time
Do not convey,
The past that lives in the present

Today, life is more peaceful than the yesterdays
Of eras times five.
When women worried on husbands' returns
And mother's 'nightmared' the years
From toddler to teenager to manhood

Here whatever the occasion
Birthdays, weddings, funerals
Always funerals
Even a small jovial gathering of some
An open bottle and heads full of memories
Is when the old songs
Will colour the air.

Orange. Here
Green. There
Lyrics of martyrs, rebels, the fallen
So many innocents pushed from this time and place.
To where time has no meaning
And the place is from where there is no hope of return.

All of this she thinks.
Every day,
Every day
When the shower starts a cue to her son singing
Frank Sinatra lyrics
That make the heart of his Irish mother
Simply smile.

IN HONOUR

They were beautiful.
Not all of them,
Some of them.
A few of them, most of them.
Were beautiful.
And they were pure,
Well some of them,
Quite a few of them,
But not all of them –
In their hearts and souls,
And in love.
Not some of them not most of them –
All of them.
And because they were in love
They were blind to anything else –
All of them, most of them,
Yes most of them.
They had dreamt of love,
They dreamed love,
And now they thought they had love.
All of them, not some of them, all of them.
And so they saw no wrong,
Not one of them.
For here was the perfect man for them –
No matter what the flaws of looks or stature,
Here was their man and that's all that mattered,
To all of them.
Well most of them,
Some of them.
So one or two got caught unawares –
Over-enthusiastic to surrender,

And too late they realised a period had been missed.
But not all of them –
Some of them,
A few of them,
But for the rest
It was marriage
And wedded bliss.
Or was it blisters?
Blisters of hate,
Blisters of rage,
Blisters of agony,
Blisters of racism.
Not for a few of them,
Not for some of them,
For all of the nigger lovers.
And that's what they were called –
All of them,
Not some of them,
All of them.
So mothers disowned daughters,
And fathers kicked them out,
Whilst sisters ignored them,
And brothers spat at them –
Lots of them,
Lots of them,
Not a few of them.
So came the tide of persecution
Rising on a racist back,
That thought one race to be superior –
White is better than black,
Instead of judging people as people
In a humane pact.
Love is the way to unite this world –
Don't judge the colour of skin

But the person within.
And because love was the reason,
I am here to atone
That my mother, I am proud of her,
And I would never disown
Not a bit of her,
Not any of her,
I loved all of her.
I am a Black woman and
I am proud of what I am.
My mother came from Liverpool
And my father is an African.
I am the Mixed Race child of their relationship,
And I know for a fact that they loved all of me –
All of me, every bit of me.
No one will erase the memory that I have
Of slavery, oppression and racism by white hands
But there's one thing I learnt and yes it was from my Mum
That all white people are not the same.
So I couldn't hate all of you,
Impossible to hate all of you –
Just the racist bigots
And I know
Who you are.

AROMA OF MEMORY

There are ladies of a certain age
Their hair coiffured
From silver grey to wig black
And the corn role of childhood back home
That I hug
I smile, lean in
Wrapping my arms across shoulders
Once held straight
Letting my hands travel the back curve of years
I breathe deeply the heavy perfume
Of clean living
And a scent unnamed
That lingers in the smartness of their clothes
In this moment
I am like a young buck
Tempting this loveliness with
Guile and flirtation
Words that in their speaking
Wash away the years
To rekindle the full bosom
Of youth
They giggle at my innuendo
A little naughty never rude
For I am not church
No Miss name falls from my lips
To me they are
Sweetness
'Sister of Joy' to the vision
On a dull English morning
They are
'praise to heaven' for crossing my path

And the wickedness of accusation
That I have caught them heading sly to a discreet liaison.

My lips are now heavy with face powder, coconut lotion
Sometimes plain Vaseline
And I have to avoid tasting them as I
Tut-tut-tut my way through this brief conversation
And as I leave
Waving away the greyness of the day ahead
I wonder if they will always be in the aroma of my memory

THE CHAIR

my mother
as canny as any purse
empty Wednesday wages Saturday
took a fancy to a pink upholstered Parker Knoll[19]
sat lounge elegant furniture floor Lewis's[20]
turned to me and asked for the loan of a cheque
me as solvent as a giro-fortnight
indicated that rubber might have competition
if i let one go
but she promised
putting the insurance man back one week
and deferring the catalogue
that the cash was as good as mine
so i go automatic party planning
and forget to conceal the twinkle of ready money coming my way
thus tipped my mother which sent her bypassing my hot palm
to the bank clasping readies
and with no account number was asked by the teller
(pre-computer days)
for the colour of...
Black she cries
indignation rising
and she's my daughter and i love her
but Black politically-racially you wouldn't understand
her red hair she gets from me
Mixed Race you know
not half of anything
a whole beauty of Black womanhood
do you have a problem with that she asks
embracing the whole queue as her audience
no he says turning a tinge bit 'coloured' himself

we know she's black he says
but her account is that in the red or black
we need to know to find the number
but my mother didn't assist
but fled,
a bit red
so the chair in the end came free you see
'cos the cheque bounced

JONESING

32 hung curtains on day they wed,
Never washed them,
Never drew them.
From 44–53 they hung stiff
Like old oak tree.
Then frayed
Rooted into the floor
And holes disappeared
'Till there was nothing at all.

Mrs Duncan could clean nothing.
Washed her frillies Sunday morning,
Smoothed each crease with electric ironing,
So by tea time wired in place,
Whiter than white, hung her lace.

Crochet weave and blanket stitch
Thermal cover at 26
Better wool than striped sheet
Shamed the neighbours of our street.

But no one could beat my mother –
Curtains hung in every colour.
Birthdays blue, green for Easter
Not a season could defeat her.
Windows crackled shining brighter
Bleach-white lace that glowed at night.

And how those housewives despised her,
Stoning steps their mouths chastised her.
Jonesing was one of life's facts –
But not when Jones was proud and Black.

PARENTS

My mother washed clothes as a hobby
a virtue
passing long days upper floor Berkeley Street
Outside
men waited long shadows of themselves
in the light of the day
In silence they told of other places
where lampposts were tall trees
and traffic rustled four-legged through bush grass
Cleaning up was a ritual that united my parents
washing up as he scrubbed down
her pinny, floral a bright contrast to
the navy blue-below-decks
where he sailed the seas
My father was ever restless
turning tidal in his search for a shore called home
every dock was temporary
every harbour a pause in his journey
This man came from rivers of stout fish
and escaped poverty
to the destitution of manmade canals
where he never sailed in harmony with life
and so
She worried on his return
picking up pennies of labour
from a hand dirty with oppression
And feared
always
that one day he would simply jump ship
to join those still floating a middle passage
between here and there

and in the still night she would listen
as the sea wailed its warning
Once all of this was mine
Once all of this was mine

THE KITCHEN

I've taken to lying down in the kitchen
Not by the cupboards and cooker
But the other end near the dining table
Where the two chairs often face each other
At a weird angle off centre across the floor
Here on velvet cushions in blue, the deepest red, gold, yellow and green
I can see the length of the garden
Watch the newest intruder a stout ginger
Entering via the broken gap in the fence the fox also uses
I see the squirrels dash along their tails flicking as they scramble
Sometimes too often they descend to plunder and ravage
Seeking to find hazelnuts they buried and forgot where within seconds.
Here lying at a slightly awkward poise
I begin the day amazed
By the before and after of 'Homes under the Hammer'.
Then 'A New Place in the Sun' eases the afternoon in
This is where I sleep
Losing time to get through a day that seems longer
As the week moves from last weekend until shit it's Friday again
I make food and leave half cups of tea to stagnate
Tomorrow is a promise I can't make myself it will not be different
But there again maybe it will rain

THOUGHT FOR TODAY

Today I thought
I could kill myself
go to bed early
get up late
Today I'll stay in bed
I thought

Today I could wash my hair
Not wash my hair
I'd love to be bald
I thought

Today I will be different
Start my diet
go for a run
like f*** that would be fun
I think I'll order a takeaway

Today I going to get dressed up
Do my nails
To match as I paint the town red
First I better stop biting them
I thought

Today I have so much energy
I'm exhausted
I better go to bed
And delay all plans
until tomorrow

HANDS 2

I have wrung my hands
Soaked them in dishwasher
Cleansed them in the weekly wash
Of every Monday, Tuesday
A few extra things Thursday
Just the sports kit Friday
And nothing for church late on Saturday

I have sizzled them over frying pans
Singed them with the Sunday roast
And blistered their tenderness at almost every meal time

These hands have slapped out in the temper of concern
The sudden disappearance on back turned
They have smoothed brows
And wiped away tears
Over and over again

Late evening they have tucked themselves under an armpit
Or kept warm over the right never my left breast
They have sought out love
And been the security of simply crossing the road

Now I look at them
The nails are strong but plain
The palms still determined to be useful
So I wonder why
They move almost on their own
To hold my face and hide it as I cry

FEELINGS

How do you feel? I feel kinky
Like pushing you on the sofa –
And kissing you all over.
How do you feel about that, hen?

I've got this right pain.
A throbbing here by me ribs.
The old fella says it must be me heart
I say's you're joking aren't yer?
My old ticker hasn't felt a thing
For the past five years –
Since your last affair with that wee hussy,
God preserve us.
You'd think men would get a bit fussy with age,
But no –
Where's there's no sense there's no feeling.
Now ain't *that* a cliche?

Been reading in my newspaper
About this Asian fella battered by a gang of youths
Red like a scrag of meat he was.
Doctor said he wouldn't have felt a thing after the first blow
But makes you think, you know.
And that wee Lass
Raped unmercifully,
She'll have no feeling left now.
Then there's been an earthquake
Somewhere, far away, hot I'll no wonder.
One huge landslide –
So many zeros after the five
I couldn't pronounce it.

Said the victims
Wouldn't have known what had hit them
Not felt a thing.
Sucked under,
Turned numb and suffocated.
I said to our Jack –
Makes you want to count your blessings,
Thank your lucky stars –
I mean how do you feel?
I feel F-ing useless

I awoke to silence. Silence so great that in the end I left the house and went in search of people ordinary people none of whom surprisingly were Black and it was not an intentional decision but they were close enough to walk to and I need to walk through the snow before its crispness was abused by fouling dogs and people. I ate almost force fed begged to share food and I did some bland and disgusting or so vegetarian earthy that my bowels weighed heavy and ached through the night in an urgency that my inners could not or would not release. Coming home I saw numbers on the answer machine and asked myself what is this day, confused for a moment that normality had returned and the phone rings resumed automation. When I listened the voices were warm friendly loving and concerned they spoke in Patwa English French they were the rich Black voices and high-white and they spoke un-beckoned I became spirited and busy found myself washing windows at 1am. Clearing out cupboards and drawers and smiled to myself how so much like my mother I am. So I awoke today feeling good woke easy said if money was on the shelf how good it would be to live like this. I smiled at the image in the mirror ignored bulges did not even attempt to consider them ugly or lovely turned on the machine to hear again you tell me smugly no one is perfect no one not me not you and that made me smile and feel stronger so for the year ahead let's make mistakes together.

A RELATIONSHIP

I consider it a sign of our maturity
That in the beginning we saw no need
To set down the rules
Of this
Our relationship.

That early intensity –
Brief chats over the lines
That stretched into hours;
Making plans
Arrangements
That we both knew we would keep,
And dress especially for the occasion.

I recall how my smallest mishap
Was received by you as an announcement
For major surgery;
And your snuffles
Sounded to me like a virus
For which there was no known remedy

Had one of us been older,
The other younger,
I doubt that we would have come so far,
Lasted this long,

Do you remember how hurt I was
When you shut yourself away that summer?
I rang everyone:
People you had introduced me to,
People who I was loath to admit

Knew you better, longer.
When you emerged
From early to bed,
Late to rise,
I grasped the courage to tell you that I loved you.
And 'me, too' you said,
'Me too.'

That first year was glorified
In my ability to speak of us, as 'we'
A unit,
Secure and inseparable –
And still we allowed each other our own space.
So that when you were no longer available
On the frequency I was used to
I told myself that ours was a modern relationship
But I was beginning to wonder.

Was that a flicker of impatience
I glimpsed in your eye
As I retold my recent tale of woe?
But your advice told me
Just how much you cared –
And no I wasn't expecting too much.

We still made our plans
Plans for a tomorrow
That at first never dawned for you
Then I too began to play the game
Set, match.

We have never quarrelled –
Well not really,
But seems now the silences
Grow from days into weeks

Seems to me had we had rules,
Said 'expect no expectations,'
Said 'friendship like love
Does not always last forever;'
Seems to me
Had we done all that,
I wouldn't need to be asking
Where our relationship is going
Of you:
My bestest, bestest friend.

WEBSTER STREET[21]

What grand buildings schools were
Red brick monuments to learning
Tiles faded from ivory white to yellow staining
Sticky handed children joining nervously
Classes larger than family gatherings
With too many faces to remember

Over the years
Here adults disguised as teachers
Ruled the world
With canes of palm slaps
For those who did not obey
Understand or learnt
The day's teaching

Maths in rotation
Between English
And the only history
That mattered
Britannia ruled the waves
We won the war

Yet peace never found
Its place
Behind the doors of
High glass rooms
Where aromas strong from
Yard toilets
Mingled with cabbage dinners
Winded stomachs of one good hot
Meal a day

Out spewed
Labour apprentices tied by three years
Lower wages till time served
Shop girls,
Machinists before marriage and kids

The few who sat first row
Not because of behaviour
They changed one class for another
School became colleges
Universities
Working class gained middle class aspirations
Of achievement

Only the schoolyard
Truly remembered
How it all began
When the gates opened
And some ran
Some cried out of fear in protest
For their first day at school

SCHOOL DAYS

Sophistication came when all-over bottle green
was replaced by
grey pleated
with fine knit, high buttoned, hide-the-tie cardigan.
Changing from sensible lace-ups for casual wear
with the slightest hint of a heel
completed the transition from girl to womanhood.
Well, young womanhood.
Now morning bus embarked
travelling in a cost suitable for a typing pool
possibly cosmetic sales
The day no longer held the shame of only being a child
as I glided with the grace of knowing my place in the world
towards the brick fortress of how many thousand days before escape
and life
But still the journey was not easy
There were horrors that waited to abuse
First the council estate
Then the boys' gate
Led by the red headed I-wouldn't-touch-with-a barge-pole
I suffered the humiliation of a lurching fool
stiff legged
hoping in front, behind, side along my side
in showing mimicry
and wonder why I was subject to this performance
For no one mention the word disability

JUST SLOW[22]

I am not an idiot, I'm just slow.
I'm not stupid, I'm just slow.
I can look after myself and I do
But my mum's a good cook, what would you do?
I'm not an idiot.

Sometimes, when I'm not thinking,
I start humming
I think I'm singing,
But I don't know the song.
Hum hm, Hum hm, Hum hm, Hum hm,
People say, shut up that's horrible.
But so's picking your nose at traffic lights
And I never do that. I'm not an idiot.

There are times when I'm eating and not thinking,
I drop my food, miss my mouth,
So do you
That's what serviettes are for, I know.

There are some people who think I'm funny,
Think I'm a comedian.
Laugh at me. Fancy laughing at someone for no reason
You'd have to be an idiot to do that.
Wouldn't you?

I watch people, all people,
All the time.
And there's some really funny people
Sometimes I just stop, mouth open, wide eyed.
Can't believe what I can see

Thankful that I'm me.
Slow, but not stupid.

I've got a boyfriend and I love him,
And he doesn't smell,
And he hasn't hurt his head either.
We're getting married
And after our wedding,
We'll be the same as everyone else.
Cos we know,
Only fools fall in love.
You see
Slow, but not stupid. Thank you.

If you stand quiet in the meadow
It is not the voice of an Angel that surrounds you
But the wailing of those beneath your feet
If you walk the cobbled street you will not hear
The laughter of children playing
But the sound of bare feet as they stumbled from factory to school
History is not the story of common people

Hidden away by the tall cotton mills built by man
The same men who threw up tenements without water to drink to clean
Where sewage flowed amongst and between the horrors of their lives
Here existed – for this was no life, the poorest of poor
Invisible unwanted outside their fourteen-hour day toil
Common folk, a labour force of families –
Mothers, fathers, and children
Whose small chests choked on fibres that filled the air and blinded their
  eyes
While hands large enough and small,
Scavenged cotton so that little was lost for the master merchant.
England's Empire cared nothing for the human cost
Black skin was property to the plantation
And her own poverty stricken were the worker-drones of the Queen's
  hive
How Manchester embraced this image of hard labour in her coat of arms,
  the bee –
An emblem of industrious loyalty to Queen and country.

But a swarm of bees is dangerous
A deadly threat to the lives of those who exploit them
So, leave a little honey
Like the offering after Confession a small donation

Charity to keep the devil away
With little care for what has been done
For it can be done again tomorrow

Without war you need pestilence
For the lower classes will breed uncontrolled
And as they multiply,
They will look at their lot so small compared to the affluent,
Well-heeled and wealthy squanderers.
Prosperous from the honey they'd harvest from the bees
As they and their children starve

Time passes and slaves uprise –
Rebels are crushed but rise again
To break chains rusty from daily use
And the lash has torn too many backs to stop a fight for freedom.
Peterloo is testament to the dangers of a little education
The three 'R's of Rebellion, Riot and Revolution
That sent Mancunians out into the streets for their freedom
To vote to eat and make a decent living,
Diminishing, erasing the blood tainted profit for Empire and Queen.

Heed Sankofa – reflect on the past
Of our shared history

Where once rooftops were shadowed by Victorian red brick
Blackened by the smoke of those 'dark satanic mills'.
Is now a bright skyline of triple pane steel high-rise

The corridors of ragged schools no longer belch out children cramped
100 to a small room dark without light or ventilation
Today education goes beyond the three 'R's of
Reading, writing and arithmetic
The chalk and slate are antiquities long forgotten

As technology is the forerunner to learning
The city prospers proclaiming its success across the globe
It speaks not of food banks
Of streets lined with charity shops
Of those so poor their teachers ask for shoe donations
Where beds are gifted so that the young may rest
These are this century's neglected, disadvantaged, poor and depressed

Remember the forgotten for generational curses are motivated by trauma
Anti-Social Behaviour Orders. Education suspensions
And permanent exclusions
Are easily exploited as County Line recruits
Identified as villains.
Criminally profiled, wrong place, wrong face
School uniform strip searched
Falsely accused.
Exploited and groomed

Let not our youth find solace in drink
Self-medicate the anguish of their lives
Let not parents read their children's eulogies –
Death's final blow by gun, by knife, by suicide,
Let not their generation epitaph be –
They did not grow old
Their lives did not matter

If you stand quiet in the meadow
It is not the voice of an Angel that may haunt you
But the wailing of those buried beneath
If you walk the cobbled street
Your imagination will not hear the laughter of children playing
But the sound of bare feet as they stumble from factory to school
Never to escape the bed bugs, cockroaches, and dysentery squalor

These are the lives that did not matter
For history is rarely the story of common people

Raised in love, we gift you our children
Respect them.
Their culture, heritage, and knowledge
Will make local-global in this city of my birth
Tomorrow can be better.
Now the empire is over,
The Commonwealth is fleeing the Crown
And Victoria
She's long dead

Long live the Queen

THE PUBLISHER IS THE POET[24]

I look at you
And think
With despair
Borne out of affection
Why
I have missed so much

Mischief sits on your upper lip
Wisdom in your chin
And elegance is the essence of your mind

I imagine
Not with a lover's regret
Time past is gone

Forever
Is too long for a lifetime
And if only belongs to
Wistfulness

Yet if only
In the eighties
When maturity opened its arms
You had been there too
To embrace me in welcome
So, the nineties would have been
As naughty as middle age should be

STRANGE HABITS

Sitting here in the Grand Place
Brussels, Belgium
Cornerstone of Europe.
Eating chips,
Pommes frites avec mayonnaise.
I think of my Auntie Josie
and my mother's embarrassed disdain,
Really Josie,
Chips with salad cream?
You are something, you are!
Strange habits for someone who never flew

THE BLONDE

I could try to write a poem
On the theme of
The Blonde,
The Black man
And the flat tyre.

I could describe
Her nymph like figure,
And corn blue eyes.

I could then compare
His dark hue
And muscular frame
Moving in right on cue.

I could try to question
Why he crossed the expanse of the street.
Jeered by his mates
in their dicky bow ties.

I could try to explain
Why this Black Galahad,
Seemed so glad,
To be of servitude.

I could refer to
The history of our oppression
And their white blonde supremacy.

I could attempt to analyse.
And reach conclusions.
All based on racism.

I could, except –
She had neither the strength nor knowledge
And the tyre was flat.

So as there was no conspiracy
There is no need for poetry.
It simply happened, just like that.

THE BARMAID

I work here, clear tables, empty ashtrays, stand and serve, pull pumps.
Rarely speak, idle chat. Evening, being served are yer?
Can't wait for answers, rush and serve end of counter,
Evening, it'll be the usual I'll be thinking
Gives him a chance to pinch my bum,
Ee you are a right one. Bet his wife doesn't give him one.
Tell she's got her head screwed on.

Now he's a sweetie, always well dressed,
Not like the rest. Drinks G & T.
The real kind of man for me.
I see your boyfriend's late again?
What you need is a real woman like me.
Don't worry darlin',
I'm only dreaming.

Pint of bitter I know, I know.
You don't know what you fought the war for, England's going to the dogs.
What did you say? He says it's full of 'poofs and wogs'.
You're blaming it on the Who? I thought the real problem was you.
You've never done nowt since you hung up your khaki
And now you say, Who? Oh my God he says It's the fault of the Pakis.
Sorry I've no time for that there's a bloke here dying of thirst.

Same again ladies?
See this one she'll be sick in the loo
Had three Bacardi now she's on that Pina Colada
And hark at her toffee-nosed cow
She's feeling smug now but wait till her hangover in morning

Oh my God, students,
Sorry no coke. You'll have to try the youth club.

Oh, you're from the university!
Well it'll have to be a Perrier won't it or else go thirsty?
What you're studying for a degree you know what worries me?
You could end up running this country.

A pint and a half,
And three whiskeys, in the same glass
What, you don't know why she left yer?
Is it such a mystery?
You're a piss head,
Just like the rest.
And don't tell me
They should have won on Saturday

Oh, I used to care,
Style me hair, red lips.
'course I was as thin as a stick in those days.
Wine bar, very smart,
I've pulled some tips in my time.
First, I did Friday then Saturday
And Sunday lunch
Soon Monday, Tuesday, Wednesday.
Now I'm here. Up town, downtown.

I work here. Clear tables,
Empty ashtrays.
Stand and serve.
Pull pumps.
Rarely speak.
Idle chat.
Evening.
Being served are yer?
Can't wait for answers
Rush and serve end of counter
I've got no brains as no doubt you can see

BOYS NIGHT OUT

He was going back in the morning.
To the whole gafuddle.
Wife and kids.
So why not?
A night out with the boys
Is what he enjoyed.

The company of men.
Drinking, singing. –
Those lyrics.
Sweet Mother of Mary, –
They'd make a grown man cry.
He'd ended up many a night,
Blabbering like a baby,
His arm thrown over the shoulder
Of another git,
More drunk than him even.
So invited or not,
He was going.

And he wasn't invited.
He had sensed the thrill of a plan.
He could smell a party a mile away
As his throat parched in anticipation.
No married men, they'd said.
Too risky.

So there had to be women.
Slags.
No doubt Brits.
And he'd never had one.

So here was his chance.
That would shut the old woman up
And the mother too.
Not that he ever spoke to her.
Always accusing,
Pressing him to confess sins
He'd never even dreamt of,
Till tonight.

Tonight,
As he crept like a fugitive
Down dark streets piled high with sand.
Searching for clues he hadn't really heard,
Or understood.

Turning he saw them,
Huddled and crouched.
And as his voice broke the air in greeting
The flash came bathing over him
Like no dawn ever had.

He was going back tomorrow
To the whole gafuddle
Wife and kids.
Going home,
In a coffin.

HANDS 3

i watch the elegance of hands that spread themselves in expression
those fingers which i take in my mouth
weave deep sensations as they pass my lips
i long to look at them
to study closely each line
smooth not gutted into the skin
but even this is forbidden me
in this moment of intimacy
those same hands
have at times cut the air with anger
and in their movement have threatened something
not violent in itself
but possibly worse
to erase me out of place and time
now they lie idle
not bothering to cohort themselves
in the myth that unfolds each evening

THE VISA

As before
She steadied herself
Body weight on the ball of her foot
Had she been a tripod
Her right leg was the first
Both arms the second
Her left leg the third
And her body the nucleus,
Centre target.

Strange
She held her breath
And at the same time
Took massive gulps of air
And held them in the balloon
Of her stomach
Forcing the swell of her skin
To tighten itself
Into a shield
Ready for rampage

With closed eyes she watched
The manoeuvres
And thought of vermin
Darting forth
Nostrils flared for the stench of its prey
Whiskers like visible twins of a tongue
Eager to dip, lick and swallow

The weird thing is
She could hear the silence

It pounded against her ears
Louder than all the chaos
The TV had stopped screaming
The cups, plates, dishes weeping
The chairs sobbed prostrate

For the briefest second of a second
The ball of her foot
Left the floor
And if watching
You might have thought her head nodded
But she was still

For the briefest second of a second
The ball of her foot
Left the floor
And if watching
You might have thought her head nodded
But she was still

For the briefest second of a second
The ball of her foot
Left the floor
And if watching
You might have thought her head nodded

But she was still
For the briefest second of a second
The ball of her foot
Left the floor
And if watching
You might have thought her head nodded
But she was still
For the briefest second of a second

The ball of her foot
Left the floor
And if watching
You might have thought her head nodded
But she was still

Then the ball of her foot lowered its heel
And the arms secondary in their position
Held firm if not firmer
So that the stomach swollen
Like the resplendence of early motherhood
Made ready for the first kick
That landed
On the third lash of her left eye
Splattering the side of her nose
It ran like a stream
Of obscenity into the corner
Of her mouth

The applauds started slow
Like the impatience of a bored audience
Then speeded to a high crescendo and stopped

Thank you he said

Thank you for what?
His voice louder
The words menacingly slower
For my visa she said
To the turn of his back
As he zipped his flies and left

SEX, LOVE, RAPE

Naturally I knew about sex
                    The street was dark, he grabbed me by the neck.
Virginity gone at sixteen, innocence fourteen.
                         The bushes were spiked like needles.
Sex was clumsy, fingers fumbling at buttons.
                         He ripped my blouse open.
Faked heavy breathing, it was expected.
                    Gagging on dank, putrid air that was his.
At eighteen I knew better what I and my body needed.
                              Those sticks of wood
                    Thrown carelessly over his shoulders
                              Are my legs.
The immature guided the inexperienced towards ecstasy
                    My skin burned under the coarseness of his hands.
At twenty, love finally bit me.
                         He thrust cruelly into me.
I chose my men for themselves, not what or who they were.
                         The sharp pain of penetration
                              I didn't want him.
Love, short term, long or not, still I experienced it.
                         He forced himself inwards and up.
My soul was given to the passing and hoped for long term love.
                    No rhythm to his deed, just an erratic thrust.
At thirty the man who was destined to be mine lay with me often.
                              Make it fast.
                    Please God, let it be over and done.
And I had need for no other.
                    Fingers tight in my hair, pounding my head.
                         His pleasure and lust, one

Love was mine.
                                        He fell heavy upon my heart
I no longer faked, sighs of satisfaction.
                        His fingers began to choke the air from my body.
Opening eyelids looking deep into the eyes of the man I love.
                                        Looking up I saw him
Shared emotion of a love destined never to die.
                        As I breathed my last I saw my rapist was also white.

BRUISED

i wish i could see things through your eyes
the rage and hatred eludes me now
cynicism is not the all of it
but the fire has gone out
and the pilot flame sput, sput like the bill ain't been paid
this is not an age thing
but the bruises that i knead in the night
throb during the day
and i am so much ailing
that sometimes i just miss the hit when it comes
and only realise i am bleeding
when that smell that speaks of blood nestles in around me
it's not that i am finished but aching really
for some peace in my life
the man done, done me in
and the man ain't always there when i'm needy
and i've been needy
how the hell do you think i got so bruised

LOVE HURTS

Bastard Bastard
I hate him I hate him I hate him
I hate them I hate them
Do gooders do gooders
They despise me they despise me they despise me they despise me
but they don't know they don't know
he loves me he loves me he loves me
he loved me
I was thin then
good looking then
I was blonde then
no patches then
I didn't cry then
I didn't shake then
No pills then
and booze then
I was fine then
he loved me then
They don't know. They don't know. They don't know. They don't know.
But I know, but I know,
not all scars show,
not all scars show,
they can hide, they can hide,
money you see, money you see, money you see, money you see,
If we had money, money.
he wouldn't hit me, he wouldn't hit me, he wouldn't hit me, he
    wouldn't hit me,
he wouldn't hit me, he wouldn't hit me.
he loves me, he loves me, he loves me, he loves me,
he does. he loves me.
really

SHE TOLD ME

she told me that sometimes
often
he has pushed her out of the bed
so that she is forced to lie on the couch
once on the floor

naked in that annex
she is like the dog in the main space under the house
when they do fuck
he does not make love
nor kiss
for he says only beautiful people kiss and she is not beautiful
when they fuck
his 'little soldier'
note the vulgarity
refuses to look at her
so he bumps her over and over
like a huge man proudly fondling his stomach as a separate entity
and he is huge now

she tells me these things
and i try to close my ears my eyes to her words
but i sense her catch her breath as she fondles herself to some level of
    passion
notice her as i count the small change difference for my own packet of
    condoms the same brand he makes her buy

once i said leave him
this is not love
now i remain silent
afraid I suppose
that her words might ricochet into my loving.

His back is not broad
Nor narrow
He is after all a real man
His shoulders are square
His Adam's apple prominent
She often watches it
In fascination
A distraction
To the demanded politeness
Of eye-to-eye conversation

She hears the movement
As he washes his hands in the air.
Even without seeing
She knows he will then travel
From his thighs to the swell of his knee
One, two, three, more
A slow powerful gesture
Massaging his muscles in readiness
Then he rises.

He is not a tall man
Not a giant
Nor is he small
And average would annoy him
And in this moment
His anger is abating

Do you still love me?
She asks
The word love

Is uttered like 'looph'
From her split lips
She blinks one eye
The right is already bruising black
And without realising
Her body folds into itself for protection
Just in case

COLOUR

The colour of his voice
Flowed cream over her shoulder
Trickling slowly down the neck
Towards her heart

As she held the air between breathing
The colour of his voice
Turned a deep blue
Of sadness
On the turn of her face
Away from his gaze

Now he knew for sure
And green like bile
Roared her back to his attention
Then his guilt could be heard
By the red of his spoken embarrassment

She hated how easily
He changed tones
Losing an argument
Meant he would gush like brown treacle

Messing up everything
She said
You know your real problem
You just don't sound black

THE DRESS

The dress had been a considered purchase
Not as some might regard a considered purchase
For she had considered the financial disaster of a debit card purchase
Considered Visa over Master (card)
Then closed her eyes as plastic slid into place
And her hand selected then finger tapped a code of hope to buy.
She had tried and retried to decide on bra and pants
Underwear that might by lamplight delight as lingerie
The dress fell long enough to bare
legs and secure heel and toe in leather straps
Of slightly fashionable fashion.
That evening minimal makeup made up
her face in timeless beauty.
Eyeliner outlined the wide expression of her gaze.
Blush found cheekbones in the fullness of her face
and her speech fell from lips rebel red
as defiant as her spirit
But today, this evening
She was coquettish
vulnerable without the armour she wore in life.
She knew the dessert of dinner would be taken elsewhere
Privacy without witnesses
And she was ready, achingly so
Feared to move in case her back might arch
Like a cat ready to spring
She wanted to be wanted
Wanted to be not simply loved
for this evening, if only for this evening
Idolised as iconic in her femininity
He lay close
And she stretched so that the whole of her

Matched exact with him
The extending of her slimming her form
To fit perfectly along his body
You know what I love most about you
He whispered
It's your thighs
They are so huge
So African
And her eyes opened to the blinding blueness of his eyes.
As her heart cracked.

MEETING YOU HALFWAY

Meeting you halfway
Seems a distance too far for me to travel
And anyway,
Your resounding cries of victory
Repeated and repeated in my ear
Would cause a revolution
Long before the ink had dried
On any treaty of peace.

And a piece of something, anything,
Would at least make it worthwhile.
Instead, almost nightly,
Flat on back, mouth open
Staring at the ceiling.
I ask myself,
What I ever saw in you.
Then you roll away and I wonder
If you ever have sleepless nights
Watching me in the exact same position.
The only difference would be
My snoring.

In the morning,
Your sneering silence of not complaining
Giving me the space to hate you
Just that bit more
As I wonder what planet you're on,
As on and on you get getting
Further and further away

I think you'll never turn back.
Look back
And remember I am here.
Over and over, I ask myself
Meet you half way
You bastard
I'd walk the moon
The bloody Sahara desert
And half the world
Cos I love you
Didn't you know that

UNBIDDEN MEMORIES

Now more frequent
Unbidden memories
Remind me where names allude
To strangers who I never really knew
Who lay next to, on top, beneath me
None of these were good enough
Or good enough to me

Often when the streetlights darken
Ready for the dawn's awake
As the vixen screeches her way along
I wake and stretch my arm
To the empty pillow next to my head
The cold from lacking human warmth
And in that moment of harsh clarity
I ask myself
Was I never good enough
for any of those men
Now estranged from me

OPEN UP

How come men always say,
Why don't you
Open your arms
Open your heart
Open your legs
Open your mind
Open your hand
Open your purse
But never, ever
Open your mouth.

OCH HE SAID

Och he said
I have the space for love to dally a night
a regular, irregularity
he who lives free loves free
And I position the sign DANGER WOMAN WORKING

Och he said
subtleties have no place
as cosmic space rushes out of global control
and I nail hammer-tuck secure the sign DANGER WOMAN
   WORKING

Taking my hand he rubs the nipple of my finger tip
until it is pert with love
Gazing he runs his eyes over the whole of me
and DANGER WOMAN WORKING glows neon bright

Smiling with just a hint of gratitude he says
You make me laugh
I like that
And I wave away caution
Remove my gum shield to kiss him full on the lips

Now it has grown dark
space is neither limited or spacial
Time has no meaning till dawn
And so it stills
And just occasionally a passing star explodes with joy
And in its glow
A lonesome eye might see the sign
DANGER WOMAN WORKING

Och he says
again he says och
As I begin my overtime.

IT WASN'T

It wasn't the first night
Of immediate prostrate
Slag jaw and wide mouth
Sensual...
Not
Sleep captures
But last night
Believing not
A better strategy to cosmetic surgery
A nine o'clock lay down
For deep slumber
To awake at times to the silence of the night
And then
Not yet dawn
Birds singing
It wasn't until the park
Seeing the school date
Laughing at the image of you
Dog chasing
That I remembered a smell
Deep in the folds of the bed covers
And my toes curl

NEVER LOOK BACK

I have travelled,
Not fast.
Moved forward.
Rested easy.
Met a brother.
Caught a lover,
Let him go
You know how love goes

Easy over.
Like blanket turning
Cold mornings.
Seeking its own warmth.
There is nothing selfish in survival.
Designed houses.
Planned homes, holidays.
Dreamed dreams.
Wiped a tear away.
Hugged sistahs.
Never looked back.
Only once, –
Only once.
Lived my life my way.

DARREN

You know how it is, sixteen,
Thought I knew everything –
Never really been kissed.
He wasn't me first.
Others had fumbled a try
In a dark corner at parties
Or on a youth club date.
But me, I was fussy
Me, I could wait.

He was dead mature –
Eighteen.
Got pissed every Saturday.
But he could take his drink,
And when he kissed me he'd dribble,
And it would run right down me chin.
He had hardly any spots,
Always wore white socks,
And had a pierced earring, just like Bros.[25]
Looked like them a bit too.
He was dead romantic.
Bought me one of them pendants and chain –
You know the type you spin
And it spells out a name.
Darren.

I was dead faithful.
No, honest. Listen –
Every Saturday night I'd get all dressed up
And wait by the phone.
So if he rang he'd know I was home.
Some nights I'd sneak out –

Eh, it was a right laugh,
And we'd meet by the back gate and he'd call me
His secret 2 a.m. date.

Once or twice he'd hit –
Just a couple of slaps,
But we always made up.
That was the nice part.

Off course, me Mam didn't like him –
But she'd never really met him.
I did point him out, one day by the shops,
But he was on his way to the match
So he couldn't stop could he?
So she didn't know what she was talking about,
Not really.

I couldn't believe I was pregnant,
'Cause we didn't know what to do –
And anyway I'd heard,
That stood up was the safest way
But me Mam knew
Right from the start.
Though I told loads of lies.
But then my skirt wouldn't fit,
Jeans got dead tight,
I was vomiting every morning,
And knackered by six every night.

The Bastard.
I told him.
And do you know what he said?
That every lad in the pub had had me,
So I could bugger off 'cause I couldn't prove it was his baby.

Me Dad went barmy.
I mean,
He really blew his top,
You know, he nearly tried to batter me
Only, our David made him stop.
Then the flippin' Social Worker
Tried to put me in care.
I was so fed up,
I didn't care.
I hated all of them.
All of them
Including Darren.
The Bastard.

So,
I decided I was going to keep my baby.
I thought, I'll show them who's a slag
I'll face my responsibility.
Only I wanted an abortion more than anything else
In the world
But it seemed as though everyone knew I was pregnant
And anyway,
Round our way
They all work part-time for the *News of the World*.
And don't tell me it's murder
Or even a sin –
Remember I was 16.
And anyway, what about him?
You can't get pregnant on your own you know.

I tried living at home,
But me Mum kept on crying
And when she wasn't we were fighting –
Blazing rows about nothing.

In Care.
Well, you know,
You're sort of all the same.
There's orphans, unwanted kids,
Thieves, absconders,
Incest cases.
Even Tarts on the game.

But you felt safe
Sorta safer than home.
You see, it's a bit like us and them.
Us girls and them staff.
Well you didn't love them,
So you couldn't hurt them –
Could ya?
Do you know what I mean?

I had six hours till me waters broke,
In a room, all alone.
They phoned me Mum
She couldn't come.
I understood –
There was me Dad,
The shame,
Oh yea, the neighbours.

But the nurses are really kind.
Did you know they called you Mrs?
'cause by visiting time everybody knows you're a Miss –
Doesn't really matter.

He's three months now,
My lad.
I've called him Darren –
After his Dad.

I want to go to college after the summer holidays
To take me A levels.
Course it's hard
'cause there's never enough money.
And me Mum and Dad do try,
But Darren cries a lot.
Nothing's going to stop that but time.

And I do get lonely,
Really lonely.
But I've grown up now.
I'm more mature,
Educated.
No bloke's going to get the better of me again.
'cause you see me?
I've gone on the pill.

MARRIAGE

The next man I meet I am going to marry
Do not think me impetuous
Or foolhardy
Marry in haste
Has always been a bad omen
I have heeded every warning
Virtuous woman always come out tops
Yet I have been on top, lots
Good girls grow to be better
My behaviour is merited in gold letters
For forty years I have tarried
So now you know why
The next man I meet
I'm going to marry

BAD TALKING

I have been cutting up rough.
Opening my mouth for North and South.
I have been standing on platforms
With my volume so high,
That they sky has had to tune in on me.

I have been
Humming and my-ing.
Cussing and sussing so many negatives.
I have cursed the devil
For his leadership.
And questioned why
The Lord has not intervened,
Then reasoned it was a problem of genes.

I have cast them all in one sorry heap.
I have floated on promises
And cursed my hopes till I've wept.
Now if only one kissable man
Would bite my tongue.
I'd be silent for days to come

BURN

heat can exchange itself
from something to keep warm
to a nasty arse trashing everything
and still licking its lips for more
many things can make toes curl
good warmth from logs crackling
or turn-on-glow-up electric flow
pay the meter heater
and fear has a tendency
to disguise itself
in an atmosphere change from deep chill
to swoon out hot
and there goes those toes again
heat deep down sensation of blood rising
and all temperatures popping
don't know anything else like it
turned the corner one day
and saw sat sitting
the most threatening god put together
since innocent got up and walked
knew right away the dangers
felt toes stub themselves trying to Jheri-curl[26]
whilst strapped in too damn sexy to walk in leather
felt but did not heed all the alarms wailing
knew blues gonna to come
told myself no life worth living without danger
birds got to fly fish got to swim and women got to take risks
why do you think Eartha Kitt got hips
so i swing mine right up and knock the guard out of the way
and sweet boy just beckoned me to sit right up

next to his glowing embers
and feel the heat
and i knew i was gonna burn

YOU GIVE ME

a small chill
a tender touch
a sense of being
the odd smile
the wide grin
the major berth
rejection
rejection
intimate moments
special days
sad remembrances
space to think
time to be
honest with my feelings
hate
laughter
closeness
honesty
morning tears
sadness
heartache
worry
questions

SOMETIMES

Sometimes you cock your head
And smile at me. –
It's a stupid smile,
A stupid smile.
And sometimes you laugh at me, –
Not with me,
At me,
Not often,
But sometimes.

Sometimes I think, –
You could cry for me,
Weep for me,
Die for me.
And sometimes you never think of me. –
Often,
Not sometimes.

Sometimes when you take hold of me –
Squeeze, embrace and lie with me.
My body aches, for the feel of thee.
But sadly now, that's only sometimes. –

Sometimes I think I am over you.
Free of you.
I'll find a love anew.
Because I know,

A sweet, sassy, sexy lady like me
Can get better than you. –
Sometimes I think that.
Sometimes.

SOHO LUNCH

I want to squander afternoons in low swung armchairs next to the fullness of a smile that begins in your eyes suspended between roof tops and the second floor looking down on traffic moving in sequence to tourists lovers so it is hard to believe that this is London the blaze of the afternoon penetrates the gloomy decor of this surprising retreat that places me within the reach of your hand and I marvel at how the stroke of your fingers on mine reminds me so vividly of love how sad that days end long before they are over afternoon meets evening like rush hour desperate to get home and long nights seem a childhood memory as the hour for demons waking signals its approach to be able to stay on through dawn needs more than this space can allow us so too early for me we rise to walk out into the still day of living and a moment's regret for not being still sixteen which would have allowed me to be swept in a passionate embrace tittering on kerbside indifferent to lumbering passer-bys thinking their tutting disapproval to be the stereo level of our lips kiss kiss but we are too cool for that too sophisticated too old to risk much more than the brush lip on lip kiss of farewell did I tell you I missed you miss you will miss you did I see sadness in your final wave goodbye.

BROSUN[27]

Thought is outside
Perceived without the perceiver
Thought is fragmented
Geography divided
Is it possible?
To look without measuring
Comparing
Thought must be controlled
Don't confuse me if I don't compare
Can I still be loved?

THE FIFTIES

My brother would visit
Doorsteps before the milkman
Collecting bottles for penny refunds
To make ends meet for our mother
Fashion was not a season
My mother experienced
Or I suspect would have tolerated
Hand-me-downs never hung
On my bedroom door
For no sister lived before me
And no one followed my footsteps
Clothes lasted

HULME[28]

Archive images confuse my memory
Of 1950s' long streets with tall green lamp posts
Beside gas lights of an era not yet passed
And trams with overhead gables led
Where buses followed

Crofts were our playing fields
Where cowboys chased Indians
And boys were boys
At war
Hop-scotch on corporation flag stones
Balls thudding against high walls
Hands felt the warmth of coal fires
Where demolition exposed brickwork
Maybe war, maybe progress.

Stick kids
In unwashed clothes
Smelt like the hops dark-clouds-brew
From Moss Lane
At dusk if you stood still and quiet
You could hear the whistle then the workers
Fleeing Trafford Park factories
Souls stamping homewards

Milk floats, coal drays and rag and bone men
Supplied nourishment, warmth and donkey stone
So my mother could hold her head high.
In front of neighbours
She bragged of a bathroom
Her own kitchen

And an unshared lime-washed toilet
In the back yard

It was rumoured that some roomed as lodgers
Living lives of get-by existence
Cooker on the landing six families sharing
Back yard ablutions
But the Christians lived in their bought
Double fronted Jamaican home grandeur
As Delvino Street expanded the Dalrymple's
Exploded out of their small terrace
Ignored by Prouse
Her one boy two girls' family unit

Here we lived
One Nigerian his wife a Liverpudlian and two kids
In a street called Radnor
That we called the United Nations
Of Poland, Norway, Pakistan and India
So Saturdays when Billy the cobbler
Got Guinness brave
His curses began with the English
Then circumnavigated the globe

OLD MOSS SIDE

When ladies would sit
Park bench
Outside the library
To watch to chat to gossip
As the hot sweat of police horses
Wafted through the air

They, summer resplendent
In striped blazers of dark hue
The fashion of the day

I remember
Across the street
Mr Finni's shop
Didn't stock anything to make a dinner of
A few old yams and cornmeal or
Garri too stale to make fou fou

Those times
Summers melted road tar
as people recall times back home
when mangoes swelled and dropped
and goats found shade on branches
too high to fetch down

While scrawny dogs
dreamed of moist meat
to relieve the hunger of their destitution

Those who drove cars drove slow to be recognised
Princess road the cat walk for four-wheel parades

Day time the Nile and Reno seemed innocent
as the Wycliffe cinema
holding fantasies and fantastic story of adventure
love loss heroism

Back then
Summer seemed to last forever
Though autumn was always impatient
Moving too soon moved into the present
scattering everywhere with falling leaves
A cloak in readiness for the coming of winter

DAFFODILS[29]

Soon the daffodils will bloom
soon the daffodils will bloom
shedding their sheaths of protection
to stand erect in their glory.

No sounds will their trumpets play
But oh how melodious
their dancing on the morning breeze.

What diligence determined their survival
in battle for life against winter
a complete contrast to the now almost
brazen contradiction of their colour
yellow for cowardice.

And how ironic
that this symbol of all that is England
should sentry this new home build
of one Nigeria
and one African-American missing.

BOLTON SAFARI

Some mornings
When October waves in November
The damp wraps itself about
Defying top level dial of central heating
Opening eyes still see the dark of night
And all that is winter clouds the mind

I know these streets
Bolton
Where no beast of four legs ever roamed
Around back yards where wild grasses
Never grew above 6 inches

Here I have never smelt ripe mango growing
Never plucked down a banana
They don't grow on lampposts anyhow
Never had red soil dust my feet

But still I remember
And on days when the wind is not chill
But warm and eager
I swear I can smell something familiar
Something not of Lancashire
And the grin on my face scares passing strangers

JAMAICAN BLUES

The only blue in Jamaica is the sky
The people are red hot delicious
Blue is for hard times
Hard times in Jamaican come regular
Like a renegade cousin sneaking to get something quick
They no work for
But blue not we
Blue came with England
Blue days of blue toes in winter
Blue spiralling hurt bad by bigotry
Long memories of blue skies left across the sea
The place where we came to after we were taken
Building shacks upon plantations
Bending low to cut cane
Looking high into the mountains
For those maroons living freestyle
Living native
Slavery turned into some kind of freedom
And then independence
But still it took reggae
Burning Spear and Marley
To re-educate all Jamaicans
So we know we is from Africa.

When you look at me now
You see the tide of time
Loss is that young girl
Who skipped through Cumberland
And fancied herself
Bringing up kin
Inna grand house on the hill
Where those with money live.

We moved here in '59
He looking for good work
A contribution to the Mother Country
Me looking for him
Waiting on the joy of children

Life's been good
Been hard
Been happy and sad when he had to leave
Not gone home or somewhere else
But leave me and the children without him

So when I look like the distance is where I am gazing on
Not true
I am studying
Seeing his ways in how they move, speak,
Hearing his laughter in the voices of the 'grands
And marvel how life keeps on linking
Generation through generation
All the way back to those African Maroons.

SOME DAYS WE ARE LIKE THE LOST

Some days we are like the lost
Spiralling between a land, a culture
A memory of a place unknown
Children born here
Still regarded as foreign

Taking trips to visit families
Arriving like strangers
Leaving full of sadness
To return to a life made secure by elders

Seeing our children hooking up with mates
As English as crumpets
Loyal friends they can depend on
If leaving here meant losing them
We can never go
And leave all of this so familiar
At times cruel
At times so wonderfully laughable

So we gather together in the rituals
Of carnival, birthdays, weddings
And to celebrate life at funerals
Clothe ourselves in our ancestral heritage
Resplendent in the knowledge
That once we were Africans
And in our hearts we still are
By the girth of our souls
The soar of our spirits
Africans abroad.

TRIO IN BLACK

She one
She is another
And me the same

When I hug them go sleep
I say a good pray
Thanking for coming so far
Not asking much but a little for tomorrow
Grateful for the day done
Safe return

Little women
I read that
Made no connection
Nice story
But little not we

From when we stand
We strong
Black women
Independent out of necessity
Reliant out of need
Strong to overcome burden
Like Amazons
Honourable, courageous, brave
And like a river
We flow continuously
All the way back to Eve
The first woman
And though this aint no Eden
Aint no Africa either
But still it's home

FOU-FOU[30] YOUTH

My father would take fou-fou
Pound, knead it
Until it formed a cloud in the bowl
For we to roll
Fingers eager
To dip into soup
Of soft meat overlaying fish
Smacking our lips on the tingle of hot pepper
His smile of pleasure
Eased out the memories
Of all the good *whuppings*
That heated our backsides for failing,
Saying, doing, something
Unacceptable to the rules we never saw written down
Now our wives
Struggle
To make again that taste of home
And delight out tongues with images of yesterday
When our mother's lap seemed as high as Mandara
And our father's voice boomed like the Niger
Today we tell our kids
To remember
They are not just Mancunians
They are also Nigerians
Descendants of Ras Finni
He who stood tall and determined for African Unity 1945
And now in 2005
We are still Africans

ABASINDI 1981[31]

The day was not normal
For days
The air was static with tension
It was feared expected and rejected as easily as breathing
Hair weaves continued
Cornrowing and stock checking
African fabric and outfits
Amongst the drums ready for rehearsals

No Facebook or Twitter existed to newsflash
But everyone knew it
Heard it
Smelt the fear felt the anger
When all exploded at 2am

This space
This haven for women and children
Now opened its arms to refugees
Of local not global despair
Welcomed the injured
The frightened
This space gave solace and protection exactly when needed

One day, July 8th, twenty-four hours
2 days July 9th, forty-eight hours
1981 Abasindi never closed its doors
To anyone

IT'S SUMMER TODAY

It's summer today
Don't laugh
Here in England
The season can change in twenty-four hours
And tomorrow might be autumn

Chorlton is buzzing
With bosoms and exposed midriffs
In competition with wobbly rolls
Of flesh without exercise

Have you ever noticed
How cool Indians, Pakistanis, Bengalis
And Sikhs are, resplendent in
The cool white wonder of their turbans
When the sun is at its highest

It has been a good season
For love and breeding
They emerge from Ikea-clad interiors
Driving the latest designed pushchairs
Murderously off kerbs into the traffic
They fuse together
A chattering
Like battery hens
The older ones trying to be more visible
Than the younger
Who always look too thin to birth
And so many of them
Missing the gold band of security

It amazes me
Me who knows so many
That on my daily journey
Home to Barbakan
Barbakan to Longford
Longford to Chorlton Water Park
Even Didsbury
I never see anyone to greet
To wave a hand
Like a flurry of flying fingers
So I talk to the dog
To accompany myself
And he is always
The most perfect of listeners

Litter is a problem
It is everywhere
Everywhere
It seems
On every surface
Every floor

I agree with the Council's latest policy
Of fining for dropping cigarette butts
I never do that
I always use the ashtray
Which I empty regularly
I have to
Out of fear it might overflow
Cascading a fountain of ash
On the letters, leaflets and ripped envelopes
Waiting on me

I've given up searching
The hope of finding your distinctive script

Telling me how you are
So far away from home

When I was a little girl
Moss Side library stood
Where the brewery has expanded on Princess Road
Summer; the two benches would seat
Neat Caribbean ladies
Ripe West Indians in freshly aired colours of home

Whilst Africans of my father's generation
No longer possessing a Dashikis
Instead remained gentlemanly
In suits with white shirts worn over,
Always over their vests.

When my father died
I gave his hat
A wide brimmed Fedora
Bought always on special order from Dunhill's
To Stan Finni
He's Nigerian also
With that patriarchal wickedness
We all have
From the Liverpool African fusion

It's really hot now
Hot, close, clammy
So that even the sun
Can't be bothered to shine
But still the joggers come
Cheap from Primark
Designer Reebok
Disgracefully short
And needing a wash

Of oh? Heavens
When did those legs last see daylight
And they can't make up their minds
Half-run half-trot stumbles of the
Ridiculously, politically, called white.

Today I am making myself promises
Resolutions
Much the same as I did yesterday
To be honest

But when this long hot
Day of summer
Finally leaves
And the sky darkens
I expect to realise
That I am once again
TV surfing for something intelligent
To stop my brain from thinking

And tomorrow
When the post lands
I will resist for hours
To retrieve it
And when a tall, tall Black man
Appears before me
I will not tell myself
It is you
Arriving Special Delivery

Maybe tomorrow it will rain
I hope so

THIS DAY

Before four has chimed,
By church bells too far away for hearing
For me the day is over.
The night brings with it
Weariness,
That makes eyelids heavy
And the heart swell with grief.

No fire blaze can warm the spirit.
The day is done,
And the need to wrap myself
In the blanket of depression
Forces legs into action
And knees to bend and stretch
Upward towards the safety of bed

Yet even the knowledge of winter
Has its surprises
When no clouds are visible
And blue is as vivid as a Mediterranean sky
High above the bustle of Manchester

Parks become an oasis of beauty
Where trees barren of their haute couture
Hold a certain beauty as the sun twinkles out of reach

Squirrels, ever cheekier
Move in closer
Preening, posturing, posing.
And birds retell their stories
To anyone who takes the time to hear

Now I forgive her
England!
Forgive her dark dullness
Her frosty nights
Her cold chills and foggy wrapped dampness

Now this home feels like a good home
And I smile at others who have ventured
To be close to this possibility
Summer has not gone forever
She is simply waiting, patiently,
And in expectation of her return
I find the energy
The bravado
To let four sneak past
Until eight, nine even eleven
Cannot make me believe
That this day is done.

4AM

It's 4am and snowing
cold the cold of UK winter
We engine stall to watch a fox confuse wasteland for forest
on a stranded corner between terraced and semi-detached
This has been a rare night Australia red wine diversity
allowing for slack jaw talking
that swings wide open
on discovering my 150 tow-charge of police clamping
and so we move in revenge of legality to the gay bar
onto working-girls saloon
seeking something we were neither looking for or needed
to end searching a bookcase for titles known
but not yet discovered
finding instead photographs videos of our past
feeling guilty that all evening you held topical
amongst those not experienced enough to be bored by your name

HOME

Cleo is home when I wander
to far places
in this strange country
that longs for me to be far away
to where home is
a bright smile of welcome
in a buzzing throng of people
who never call me stranger
and never ask
where do you come from
but who would feed Cleo
if I left England

THE SOLDIER'S DAUGHTER

A Force
Marching in lines
On parade
Spick and span
Crossing miles
Rarely at ease
Till in the air freedom
I never learnt to fly
Never grasped the drill
Wanting to rest for a while
In one place
Any place and call it home
To say these are my friends
My school
My street
My anything
But everything was theirs
Do not touch signs hovered
Above blank stares
And I heard them whisper
There's the new girl

CHEETAH AND STAG WITH TWO INDIANS[32]

This my friend is a circus
This green land and rolling hills
Are simply back-drop
To a stage struck for our performance.
As the trap is set.

Come perform your trickery.
They have come to be entertained
Ignorant and uncaring of your majestic survival.

They respect no beast but themselves.
See no jungle in their own heart.
Call we natives in an alien land.
And pay our purse
With the gold of our ancestors.

OTHELLO[33]

Take care for though I look away,
I sense you prey on my soul.
I turn away to see right through
Your camouflage of friendship.
Brush and canvas whisper conspiracies
For my ears only.
As paint sterns my features
To conceal my smile of knowing,
Canvas flexes like muscles
To restrain my presence.

Image is captured,
But not my spirt,
Not my soul.

It doesn't matter what you call me.
No name – no man!
Blackamoor, negro.
For you must paint me Black,
And my people will know that I lived
Despite curious exploits;
That I played on stages of life,
Trod boards of existence
And they will applaud the actor of me
As they salute the man in me
And call my name
Ira – Africa!

WOMAN AND ELEPHANT[34]

I ride on the back of elephants
A colossus between my thighs.
I sit high above nature
Only the giraffe can see the glint in my eyes.

Together we gallop along in a thunder
Trampling underfoot.
We forage on nature
Ripping food from its roots.

I ride on the back of elephants
Because men have not the girth.
Men are too busy discovering the universe
To realise, –
Women are stranded on earth.

FOR GORDON BENNETT ABORIGINAL ARTIST[35]

Home has no place in my house
for it is not here where I live.
Situate me in front of a winter fire
flushed with electricity, gas – hot
and see if you can,
the blue hue chill across my face

I walk confidently through streets I know so well
appearing lost in my travel
between here and there.
For here is not where I am
and there is not where I am going to.

Seated or standing
my body bends to a wind of change
that keep on blowing through me.
Right through me.
So my existence struggles against gales from the west.

My life is so full of living.
Day by day.
Yesterday for tomorrow.
Tomorrow because of yesterday.

The success I have in grasping humanity
out of your savagery.

Late and alone I listen to my ancestors
and their spirits guide me so that though home
Is not the house I live in
living is the life I have

L.A. SEASHORE

i wonder if it will haunt
the decay
the odour
will it stay with me to mar
all my memories of this day
bright
hot but not steaming
walking easy across scratch grass
to slight slope
stepping down onto seashore
fresh sand lacking footfalls
no sign of anyone
here among tall rocks and virgin surf
breaking easy
here
a moment of sharing intimacy
telling stories
stating opinions
here
forgetting the day to day of day to day
will this memory fade
unable to break through the sight of the bulk
rotting no longer flesh
stench of sea lion
hugely dead

TESTING THE ANGER OF THE SEA[36]

It was not that it has
A European bias
It held no interest in
The land
Where political bigotry
Found support in votes
Of an ignorant, racist electorate choice.
It was not concerned with
Climate change
Though it watched the clouds.
Or droughts in rain forests.
It went where it wanted
It welcomes the thaw of snow-caps
That finds its way
In a slow flow towards its embrace.
It is true, it could be a sheer delight
Of refreshing calm in a summer afternoon
Full of clear blue skies.
Or in winter when it moves silent and unseen under ice
Its laughter swells as it rains.
Swallowing and expanding
Until it finds its climax in a storm
So why when all humanity has denied them
Do they continue to risk
Testing
The anger of the sea

STRANGEWAYS[37]

What did you think as the roof flew high
And smoke began to billow and rise
Let it burn
As long as there are no casualties
In this hell of depravity
That has no morality
Let it burn

Here there is no humanity
That lets men live in insanity
Christ is there no charity
Burn, burn, burn.

We have a price to pay
And we pay each and every day
But how much can we pay
It's got to burn.

This is where the beast hides
In some he has laid down and died
But other beasts bide their time
For freedom.

But he who turns the lock and key
We recognise the beast in he
Behind his uniform revenge is at liberty
So let the bastard burn.

These are not strange days
This is the life in Strangeways
In hell it burns everyday
So this F-er's got to burn.

THE SCREW

It's the shoes that give you away
Scruffy shoes, dodgy bastards.
Take trainers, wouldn't be seen dead in a pair.
Manmade textiles!
You could brush them till your arm dropped off
And not get a hit of gloss.
A good character reflected in the shine of your leather.
That's what I say.
It's natural.
Like the leather.
Enduring.
No matter what the weather.
It's like a well-oiled lock.
A smart uniform.
The lads wear pumps.
Dirty scruffy white ones.
And there's black ones. lots of them
And you'd never know if they were clean,
Would you.

I'm not a proud man.
I like simple things.
A simple life.
Could have joined the army
Gone to war
But I'm doing my bit
Keep the scum in place.
So that you lot can live safe
In a clean society
Dusting off your innocence
It's all bleedin gloss.

HE CAN'T GET OUT OF JAIL

this isn't monopoly living
before he was schooled full term
he had already doubled up tripled up
4-manned himself into space time
shuffled a line like the old days
sat dog like in a corner and whimpered
ran fleet footed before tripping
and slammed again
doing months doing months doing, doing time
no day different from tomorrow
no misery free from yesterday
stupid and walking like a zombie out on the street
searching for times long gone
brothers turning to dust since he last hung a block
feeling isolated in freedom
feeling scared in his own back yard
stumbling to make small words with those who breed him
and love him less now than before he lost the will to be
he telling tall stories of other guys' lives
trying to build himself a reputation
and when people turn to get their shit together
the only way they know how
working saving
he already planning a longer stay
a 6 to 9 or maybe 12 to 15
home
the brother wants to go home
to a regular place
where the key turns
and the door clanks
and the light don't ever go out
and monopoly is a reality for the brother
who can't get out of jail

THE WITNESS

Mornings always too quick to dawn
Even in the dark of winter they woke her.
Sitting she grins stretched lipped
And sighs for one hour, one day more.
But holding herself determined
She moves bladder tight across the hall
Then sharp relief
inhaling at the same time
the scent of her own water.
Hungry cat and dirty dishes greet her
As now her speed-up
She begins the beginning of her day wondering
if she needs to wash and groom her hair
or escape the chore for one day more.
Time flies and two hours pass before at last
she is ready.
The day holds no surprises
Brown post of theatre flyers
no bills thank God and no pay either.
Still her credit is lousy but plastic and possible
and her cheques as durable as an old Durex.
Today she moves elegantly from door to car
going nowhere
eager to arrive.
Today she tours old neighbourhoods
churning up childhood memories of a mother's love
swore friendships of a lifetime that she grew out of.
Here she stalls the engine
corner sitting,
remembering kisses and hot hands
when a youth hits her vision

And her heart leaps into her mouth
an invisible red
pumping in rhythm with the wound in his head
And no one will ever believe
that she didn't hear the bullet.
See the car.
Remembers nothing only that,
she witnessed death
and her heart refuses to recover.

BAM BAM[38]

It's a hell of a thing
When a gun come home to live with you.
Things change,
House change,
You change.

If you were the master, the man
Now you not even the bend down,
Yes sah, servant of the house.
You is the below stair
Threaten live outside
Back door porch
No good nothing
For the gun in big biggest armchair
Tapping impatience.

Gun is restless, got no easiness waiting
Waiting for chat
Gun no watch TV
Got no hunger for pizza,
Special seasoned chicken,
Tub full of vanilla ice cream
With chocolate running down
So you must lick before spooning.

Gun full already.
Belly full of cold bullets
Gun need to let one go.
Not just fart,
But one big brown one

That smell like nothing
No one who never been to war smell before.

Gun got power
Make your palm itchy when empty.
When you doing anything
Make you leave and sit and wonder
Should you take gun out to play
But gun no player

Gun got no hobby.
Gun is professional,
Born into the business
Career change never.

Gun need a target
An aim
Gun is always thirsty for trade

Clever gun make words
Speak loud in your head
Whatever you doing.
Sleeping, watch TV,
Staring out to nowhere.
Don't reach for nothing to calm you.
Weed no strong enough
H and Crack will paranoid your paranoia
So that when gun say now
You be up and going
Maybe somewhere,
Possibly nowhere
So long as you and gun be on a journey.

And the silence
The silence is so loud
You squeeze your eyes to slits
Trying not to hear
Until Bam Bam
You dead
And who die with you
Only the gun knows

JOSHUA WAILED

Joshua wailed nightly
Dog on heat
Knew the sound
And dipped its tail and whimpered
An agony silently remembered

Other men rolled
Like boulders
Heavy with age
Blown like feathers in tornadoes
Hiding themselves in small balls
Of feigned innocence

Joshua knew innocence
It lay like a smut moustache
Above his lip
And he licked it hungrily
Before every sentence
Taking huge gusts of air
That tasted like freedom

But before he could speak
The wail blew itself out
Slapping itself on doors
Walls,
Hanging momentarily
From the ceiling
Then whoosh like a flicker of a flame
It was gone

His mother used to say
His mother hadn't said shit to him
Most of his life
And his father's silence
Was only matched by his distance

Lots of people had told him
Move. Stop. Stand. Go.
There, Be Quiet.
Don't talk.
Eat.
No. No. No. No. No.

This last day
Last day
Joshua had stopped wailing
Now he held his head
Held it totally
With his hands
Wrapping his arms around it
Right up to his elbows

Something had changed
Changed amongst those closest to him
This last day
Sum total of time
24 hours
1440 minutes
They had started to whisper

He felt
Though not sure

A slight warmest almost from them
They never looked at him
But they had stopped shouting
So Joshua no longer knew
If his wails had sound
Because no one told him
To shut the fuck up anymore

Now when he ate
He found his mouth welcomed and caressed each bite
Other days his teeth had ached
And his tongue like a rotovator would turn and eject everything
But not this time
Yet, even as he realised this pleasure
One of them sat closer to him
Whispered so quietly
That the sound shocked Joshua so much
A wail almost escaped again

You ready, said the whisper
Whilst another laid hands so gentle
Joshua almost,
Almost but did not
Remember his mother

Dead Man Walking went the cry
And Joshua began his last wail.

LITTLE BOY GAWN

The little boy that I once knew,
Grew.
I do not know him now.

Memory is a framed stillness.
A pause in the video of childhood.

Three desks from mine.
Not too close for a teacher's slap
Not distant enough for her antenna
To forbidden whispers.
I study the back of his head.

I see him
Grubby from football.
Crying, but not bloodied from morning break conflicts.
Weeping the shame of snapped elastic in P.E.
The same tears we all shed in time
But quickly forgot,
When delivered the naked buttocks
Of its latest victim.

I once kissed this boy.
Not real, like movie stars do.
But to escape missing my turn
And the possibility of kissing another boy
Who never looked at me.

I had forgotten him, the boy
As I grew.
If I ever saw me he never said.

Maybe he never knew.
And passed me like any other stranger.

Of my life he knew nothing.
Of his I now know everything,
Almost.

I know the names of his children.
His mother's name.
Although I never saw her at the school gate.

The street he moved to
Not all that far from where school used to be.
And his eyes.
After all these years I know his eyes.
They stare at me.
Penetrating.
Unblinking,
Under the headline of
Murderer

HE IS A BIG BOY[39]

Yes, she said, him a big boy.
Her eyes resting on the top of his head
Then travelling
Like a grease splatter over fresh cleaned
Down his throat to rest on the flat of his belly
She blinked into speech.
His mother feed him good
Plenty fish for his brain
Goat meat to keep his body agile
Rice and peas for stamina
And sweet potato pudding so he always find a smile

Her hand reaches out but she does not touch him
But walks slowly to his side
Yes indeed him a big boy
Like a Blue Mahoe
He straight, beautiful, durable
And full of music
See his hand
Wide enough to move water
And play sweetness upon the heart

Her head turns as her tongue
Licks something only she can taste from her lips
Then they reshape into a pout
To release what seems like all her energy
In a deep whoosh of air

Her hand rises to trace the outline of his stature
But cannot move further then the narrowness of his hips
As though his thighs resist her

See them thighs she says, you don't know love
Until a man thighs hold you down
Carry you from the dryness of the land
To the warmth moistness of heaven

Big boy she says
This time almost silently
I will miss you
And she continues to walk forward
Past the coffin of her lover
And out into the stillness of the night

MY MOTHER AND SISTER ARE COMING

Three nights earlier
She had made her plan
Not the brightest thing
But capable and cunning

She had seen Lydia looking
Recognised the slime glow
Behind the eyes
Seen it before
In blue-eyed-boys
30 years plus, plus, plus
Social workers
Even the lacking trust Carers
Who didn't give a damn for her
For any of them

So the first chance she had
She had tempted Lydia
Just by hanging close
Letting her smell her
Brushing her hand
As she moved her food tray
Then raising her arms high
So the fullness of Lydia's eyes
Matched the roundness of her breasts
Nipples perked in expectation
That Lydia could make it happen
Even here
Especially here

Time found her
With one day to spare
Makeup practising
Needed, for she hadn't noticed
The darker tones of Lydia
Obvious now in the foundation of shade
Fortunately not enough
To make worse that
Which she wanted to hide
Wanted to conceal
Wanted invisible

The teeth marks were still there
Three weeks four days later
The blue bruise
Still shadowing her eye
Only the flap of flesh
Had finally said farewell
To her ears.

It was a pity she thought
They couldn't clean up her face
The way they had painstakingly
Cleaned and swabbed her hands
Her nails
Until their spotlessness
Had a manicure standard

Ta Lydia
She had lent forward
Avoiding the puckered lips
To kiss the air with her promise of
I'll make it up to you
The words leaving her mouth
As easily as her body twirled out of Lydia's reach

It's been three weeks, she said
Almost four
Feels like a year since I saw them
My mum and sister she said
Smiling now
Really smiling
Smiling for the first time
Since that first time
That only time

I didn't think they'd come, she said
Not ever.
Never
Thought I'd done it
The worse. You know.
And well…

Got to go, she said
Suddenly nervous
Luck, said Lydia
Not really wishing a future
More a question
With the unspoken words of
And you will come back later
In the dark
When the others are sleeping
Back here where I'll be waiting

By the way
Lydia's curiosity getting the better of her
Who did you top?
You know,
Bump off
Murder

My dad, she said
Stopping like stone
Turning the eyes of a Siren
Full onto Lydia
He tried to fuck me

JOHNSTON

When Johnston finally fall
He fall hard
Had he been outside
Pavement crack would be too large to repair
If he fall from high rise
No soft landing to catch that fall
If he fall from Grace
Amen from here to eternity never gonna save him
Johnston man just fall

He no trip
Me knows man can trip
But p-l-e-e-e-a-s-e
Tripping is for ladies
Silly girls in too-too high heel
To get from here to there
To where we is now
Talking about Johnston
So true, believe me
He no trip

Maybe he faint
Not swoon exactly
But change from this is real (bad)
To total unconsciousness
Like him dead
Me know he wish to be

Definitely this was no seizure
Though all eyes watching hoping
He get seized quick-quick

And no blood clot (bloodclaat)
Burst his vein
So his brain swimming like blob
Inna cherry juice

But his eye stare
Pumped out like he got new job
Alien species disguised as a man
A man, he?
Stop make me wander from this
Tale me tell you

And his hand reach up
Trying to clasp a heart
Hidden beneath design threads
No money he work bought
Covering breast full like puberty
Make you wonder how he ever
Know it was beating

Sure beating now
Not regular be-bop, be-bop
Not excited like it playing Soca rhythm
But hard like they used to drum warning
Go hide. Go hide
Ghosts coming to steal our people

But where he gonna hide now
With all who live close
Waiting, watching,
Like we done every afternoon
When man leave
Then Johnston come calling
Hands already working belt buckle

We been living anticipation
Waiting watching now done
Johnston a falling
Hear 'The Man' say[40]
I'm going to slap the black offa you
And Johnston man he start to fall

SILENCE

I can hear the silence before waking and feel the first intake
of the day knowing nothing special there shouldn't be a break
from next line

today as yesterday a child died slowly within a moment of
exquisite pleasure penetrated by the long penis of lust again
here

today a stone's throw will receive in return a bullet maybe
rubber probably not and shrapnel will disfigure a child

begging having crawled from under the city she will offer
herself to a stranger who for one moment will notice a
resemblance to his daughter then dismiss the thought with
the laughter of his pleasure to come

THE UNFINISHED CONVERSATION[41]

I am sat in a dark room watching an installation
The images hurt yet I have seen them a hundred times more
I can nightmare in the dream of them sitting anywhere

There are white people here I wonder what they see
And if there is a hurt to share from history

I have seen children in factories
Some dark with the smut of chimneys
And felt anger in their despair
But no guilt
For my hand did not rob their childhood happiness

But when my children
The great, great, great, great grandparents of my parents
Are shown shackled with blood fresh from lashings
When my father the great great grandfather of my father's
    cousin is
Drenched with fire hoses of oceanic strength multiplied
Then my anger foams in my mouth with a bile so poisonous
My soul staggers to keep my body upright
To breathe the air robbed from me
To beat the heart that has missed so many beats that
Death is already celebrating its victory
And when the earth regains its axle
I realise that this dark space of creativity
Is not simply telling a story
Images on a screen
It's retelling history
A never ending loop
Retelling it again and again and again
To stop the truth from ever being forgotten

ROSA PARKS

She tapped her feet.
Left, left, right, left.
The rhythm bore no impatience.
She simply tapped.
Left, for three: right for three,
And the beat became musical...
There was nothing strange about the day, nothing.
In fact it was the ordinariness of the day
That made it so ordinary.

Work, well her feet ached,
Her legs ached,
Her knees ached,
Her back ached,
Her necked ached from having to keep her head bowed low.
Much the same as any day.

She thought about the food she would eat
When she reached home.
Then dismissed the notion,
Knowing that the menu would not vary greatly
From any other day.
No there nothing different about this day.
Nothing at all.

There seemed to be quite a few people about.
She noticed them.
She said hello to those faces she knew,
And looked away from the faces of strangers.
Well, some of them.
Some she stared back,

Clear-eyed wide,
The way you do:
Looking, seeing and thinking about nothing at all.

When the bus came she climbed on,
And took a seat, moving now
On her journey home in the working life
Of an ordinary woman,
An especially special, ordinary woman.
It wasn't long before the bus became crowded
And people began to block the aisles.
She sat, looked out of the window,
Taking no real account of the people about her.
She sat, thought of home,
Her supper,
Her free day,
Her family,
But most of all, the free day,
When she would not have to travel the bus line:
When she wouldn't have to work till her feet ached,
Her legs ached,
Her back ached.
And her neck ached from keeping her head bowed low.

So that when the man said,
'Stand up girl I want your seat,'
That's what he said.
'I want your seat.'
The way that white people spoke to Black people
During the segregated years
Of the so-called United States of America. –

What sparked her rebellion,
Inflamed her desire for freedom and equality

She will never know.
She simply said, 'No,'
And in her mind she said.
'No I will not stand for you.
I will not stand for you.
I take this seat because it is rightfully mine.
Not simply because I got on the bus first.
But because I helped to make this seat.
I help to drive this bus.
I helped to put you in your place,
Which makes you think that you are superior to me
That I have no rights
But you cannot exist without me.
And all my forefathers.
And all my great, great, great, great, grandmothers.
I, Rosa Parks, refuse to give you white man my seat.'

OBAMA[42]

How many did not utter the words
Maybe not beyond their lips
Up inside their head
Bus travelling to work
Being served second,
First in the queue
Waiting patiently to be ignored.

I know I did,
Without hesitation.
Spoken them out loud in classroom workshops
Over dinner,
Lying close after love
And even then the fatality of them
Was tinted with the dream

I have never climbed a mountain
But believe in the principals of Sankofa
To remember is to reflect
And at the same time look forward.

So for the children of my children
Maybe,
But in my lifetime
Never!
This aint Hollywood
And anyway
When is
It's a disaster movie

Now we are working without scripts.
Every line is considered,

Punctuated with the possibilities of what is to come.
Flags getting ready to fly a different hue
Old Grandmas smiling toothless gums
And still remembering the hardships
Of those already passed
Lynched and beaten by The Man.
Never thought they'd see it

'*Not in my lifetime*'
These words have echoed over generations
And end here
In the centre of living the dream

Martin saw it
Sammy sang the harmony for Odetta and Eartha
And Malcolm determined it
By any means necessary
This new beginning
Has just begun

MASSACRE[43]

The they that kill us
Threaten our lives from dawn to dusk
Plot our extermination
In public arenas
Of council office
Self-identified churches
That are without the true God
They who claim what we have achieved
They permitted
And the rest we took
Through stealth crime
By any means necessary
Because that is in our genetic makeup
Thieves from the cradle to the grave
Sexual deviants from puberty until incarceration
And they hope no appeal death row
First they cloaked themselves in missionary cloth
Then in the wealth trappings of slavery
And when freedom brought emancipation
They donned pointed hoods and white sheets
To conceal their uniforms and shields
Who are they?
These senators, mayors, sheriffs.
Officers of the law. Ordinary citizens.
Priests vicars, red necked bigots of ordinary guys
Whose mantra kill kill kill
Divides this nation
Because the fear sits close to our consciousness
As our kids climb into the yellow bus
We travel the subway
Check into work

Lunch out
Watch a movie
Go about our business
Minding our business
Bow our heads in prayer
That as we reach out to our neighbour
He isn't taking aim

YOU FORGET THE HATE[44]

You forget the hate
In the everyday of living
Of Tesco's,
Didn't it snow
Damn the traffic and
Primark is fantastic but just too busy

You forget
In the full comfort of the Western hemisphere
Yesterday is only tomorrow's history
Where we stood at a distance
Our vision blurred by the dust of
Stomping feet charging in defiance
Retreating one hit beyond a bullet

We watched mesmerised in horror
As children bled on TV's
And the names of the missing
Were announced with the frequency
Of the weather forecast

So we stood
Some of us
Outside embassies
Walked in protest
Chanting and calling on names
To awake the Gods
Did they hear us
In time they did
In time

Meanwhile
We staged theatre
Wrote poetry
Held seminars
Debates, conferences

Looked at places of learning
And renamed them in honour of both of them
In her honour
In his name
Because their names above all others
Spoke to us of freedom
No Boers
No white supremacy
Africa for Africans

Then, as dawn turns to dust
Perfect showed its flaws
And we counted them
Like minutes into hours
Hours into days
We measured time
Without knowing
How she endured
What she endured
Counting
414 days
Without charge

There are prisons without cells
Where torture lives in the mind
Threatens the sanity
Where a door half open
Has as much terror as one locked

Love is a memory
That breaks the heart with disappointment
Because nothing is perfect
And she seemed without flaws
So that when we saw them
It scarred and scared our souls

Her halo, now dripped with blood
Down came her name
Replaced by Bruce Forsyth[45]
An educated decision I heard

Because we who did not understand
Could not understand
Murder is murder
Ask his mother
There can be no forgiveness

LANGSTON

Langston Hughes never did swear
Though he had his troubles
He had his cares.
In none of his lines of verse
Will you discover a curse.

Not once did he say
   White man
   You really fuck up my day.

Langston simply knew
How to sing the Blues
An' though his life had its miseries
He was proud to be Black
An' know that at least
His soul was free

A MIDDLE PASSAGE

It was no one particular thing
That sent me meander that lane.
Bumping, bruising, tripping.
Not one think me recall
Make me head jerk that way.

Baby fret, hold it, peace let it lie
It was much a same day.
Ordinary like tomorrow and yesterday.

Then out of nowhere salt rise.
And a stench so thick
Me hug me belly and close me eye.
And when it ease
Me vex another baby calling.
Then me laugh
For him long gone.
Long before youngest catch she own breath. –
So what smell so bad and wrap up in salt.

Then me old she dog.
With eyes grandmother-yellow
Stop to wreck me neighbour garden
Since trash boys cut off she tail.
Feared to leave me and me her
Fearing more than shit come with gas bill.
Old and feeble now.
Feeling trapped and caged like no animal ought
With legs to run free,
Did turn to me and with a look to plead, ask for death.

Was then I knew.
Was salt sea spraying
And the stench of rotten flesh, banged close
To flesh half dead.
And your eyes many Great Grandmother
look out at me from old she dog.
And see me living.

Peaceful like.
Peaceful with no desire for living
That make me stop to think
Of all who were forced to travel so far to plant me here
And me just sitting
As nasty white boys cut off the tail of me dog.
Sitting, as graffiti paint press close the walls of my home
Sitting, as looks and stares and nigger name spit travel.
And think. –
You did not travel so deep into Babylon
With lip protruding from whip lashing
To have me live a life without living.

So, I pick up me children and step out into the city street
And me head speak.
Step forward, for they cannot tar and feather you now.
Step forward, and see whose cross is burning
Step forward and start remembering
That we come from a long-lined people
This ain't no sunshine suntan.
This black runs deep.
Deep into the soul
And ain't no one going to stop this Sistah from living free.

HER STORY

Mabel stoops, scooping up water,
Skirt hitched, pailing the river;
Wipes her brow, thinks of her daughter –
And wonders if change is going to come

Martha's got clothes high in the tub,
Back breaking labour, rub-a-dub scrub:
Thinks of her Ma and prays for her daughter.
Sweat full of salt mixes with water. –
To wonder if change is going to come.

Lips pressed like mangle spitting out water,
Crushed tongue flows with blood
To mix with the water;
Prays for automation for her daughter –
Sure that change is going to come.

Deloris studies programme techniques,
Taps out a code for her washing week;
Considers herself a modern housewife,
Computer controlling how she spends her life –
Only the slave master has changed.

SAMBO'S GRAVE[46]

Sometimes when the moon is full
He pushes the earth aside
Scattering the gifts, toys, tokens
And stands on the highest point
Tip toed to extend his boyish frame
And he looks out to sea
For now he can see beyond water and land
Right to the coast of Elimna
Through the Door of No Return
And into his village and his mother's arms
And he smiles once again

THE INTERVIEW

I don't recall when it happened
but I remember the exact second,
precise like the toll of the hour and all's well
I was relaxed
teeth aching way back lower jaw.
And patient.
Paying no attention to aching collar bone, right side
and the cramp of hand, thigh, knee, calf, ankle.
My head was clear concentrating on imagery of lynched bodies,
raped women and drive-bys.
And smiling.
Always smiling.
Wanting to reach out I kept my arms straight,
hands close to my thighs
and sighed silently.
Hiccupped over an eternity of history
found my feet and walked
Well the interview was over
the vacancy had already been filled

BILLBOARD

Yesterday, saw a billboard,
red-lips-big-teeth-and-tongue-lolling
and knew that it was me
not me, but meant to be me
and not me, but we
We the people
who live on the far side of denial
Not that we deny
Our lives are one of regret
that we were ever discovered lying naked in the grass
now grass is the only economy left to build on
right through to white power
And white power is what aims to keep us
here in this place
And if not here then here
in this small place where we have no need for welfare cheques,
for our welfare is checked on the hour
or denied in a murderous moment of
who-gives-a-damn plenty more outside
In my mirror I am haunted by the beauty of my grandmothers
my head has the lineage of a man from long time past
born free and lived free
And the deep scar of my brow is the worry of survival
that lived too many generations in chains
My feet do not shuffle
but they recall at times most vulnerable
how illegal it once was to stride ahead
and it is a struggle to raise my head and look upon Babylon
These reflections carry me in indefinable battles that rage outside
    my door and creep through the cracks of the windows
Beauty I know I am for those who see.

Yet I recognise myself in every racist image no matter how abstract
and weep with the knowledge that it is meant to be me
not me exactly
but all of we.
And I call upon the ancestors to take me
for the days are too long and slavery is a choke that still possesses
only now
it is called freedom

RASTA

mild mannered like springtime
the dude
silly name for a man
but he was a dude
the dude broke thin wood flint and perched it on his lower lip
this jaunty display of manhood did not go unnoticed and he was noticed
here amongst so many
his height alone placed him higher than others
and the locks of his hair added that something special and different
but like spring
the season of new awakenings
his temperament hovered between light and dark
so that sunshine sometimes competed with the brightness of his smile
but days when autumn staggered forward for a moment
his darker side added hostility to the slightest change of temperature
he wasn't really a dude
just another brother burdened
so that history made living hard
as today planned murder for tomorrow
the brother spat out the vile nothingness of his existence
and waited for winter to come

I COULD MAKE IT ALL UP AND IT WOULD STILL BE TRUE

I don't hear your voice though I listen.
I hear you in a pulsation in my head.
The room is quiet with no music
To flow me into sleep.
And there is a space where you lie.

Tomorrow will be full of dreams.
I could make it all up and it would still be true.

Walking, I bumped into you,
A memory imaged in a coffee shop.
Hamburgers free of Macdonald's grazing.
Plump patties of English lambs to the slaughter.

I want the world to be free of blood
Black blood spilled too much already.

I want those people to scream and recoil from our history
Massacres by their hands.

I want Black men to stop dying.
I want all my Black men back.
My father, to scowl me.
My brother to sing Sweet Susie Q and smile,
His smile.

I want to hear your voice speak my name
In fun, frustration, in pleasure satisfied.

I don't ever want to stop being Black.
I will never stop being Black.

I want music in my life
So I can dance away the anger of my living.
Let the bitch live where she belongs in the doghouse.

Let me walk this world unshackled by the curse of racism
Let me not walk alone.

And if I stop for a moment
And tilt my head one side.
I am not crazy.
I just thought for a moment
I heard you speak my name.

LIVING IN A WAR ZONE

Handsome
My cousin John tells
Not handsome
Beautiful
B e a u t i f u l
Most beautiful man who ever walked
This city
The earth possibly
And could dance
Light foot three feet in the air
Michael still a twinkle in old man Jackson's eye

And style
Stylised in a fashion no-one had ever seen before
First Afro, Dread
And a voice that Bob would have envied
And Nat practised to achieve
Roots, Jazz, culturally cool
Lucky boy
Unlucky man
Living in a war zone

The Ritz sprung floor
Helped cha cha, tango and waltz get some style
Rockers to roll
Gave bounce to clumsy youth with red pimples
Now green-eyed to see this man
Brown skinned and too damn good looking
Twirling local lasses in perfect circles
Synchronised to the rhythm

How they scowled at him
And he involved with music
Danced with closed lids so his soul could hear
Did not eyeball them back
So never saw them hatch a plan
That followed him into the street
Past the hospital where I first kicked into life
Crossing over to the dark of the Palace Theatre
And forward to Princess Street near the bridge by the water

There
They took him
Pushing scrawny bodies stacking up tense
Mouths screaming savage names
From their own savage mouths
And marking the first bruises on this beauty of manhood
Grabbing now
Bits of him
An arm a leg
Grabbing his head his hair
Using everything they had to keep a hold
Teeth nasty with decay
Missing his cheek (maybe God was watching)
And found instead the tip of his ear
As a morsel for supper
That up-tempoed his footwork into a new rhythm
Faster with more deft then he had ever danced
His legs filled with the electricity of terror
And let out a roar that no Mancunian had ever heard before
Causing the ancestors to quake in memory

He pulled himself forward
But they clung, clung fast
Until arm and socket stressed

So radius and ulna left the zone of humerus
With a gunfire crack of departure
That freed him
And now his captors ran
Away
No fleet footfalls
But the stumbling falling pushing shoving stampede of beasts
No not beasts for at least they have innocence
These were demons in the face of God
The threat of daylight
Returning to the squalor of their lairs
Where George and Jack hang grey in grime covered windows
That aid to conceal the filth within

Where was his beauty now
His proud head lowered
Those arms that raised hands to clap out beats
Wave the breeze to attract a gal to dancing
Now the two hang loose like his soul
Music is a silent memory
The glitter ball has cooled its glow
And yellow lamps
Mask the dark street ahead

He senses the splash of rats
His ears still deaf with obscenities
The air is so foul
That his nostrils are confused
Sending a stench much worse
Then the decay of the canal
To sit in his stomach

His heart cries for freedom
Home and freedom

Freedom and home
A distance too far to travel
This night
Any night in his lifetime
So to Hulme he turns
Where women,
Mother and sister
Will bathe his wounds
Bind his arms
And spit out vile curses
To the enemies in the 'hood

RUNNING

Running alludes to many things
escaping enemies
relatives
situations
that kill living
Running to new things
embraces
opportunities
Running is associated with
cowardice
not facing up to
falling out of love
Running is said to be
invigorating
healthy
breathtaking
heart stopping in fright
Running speeds
walking away
walking to
distancing
nearing
moving out
closing in
losing
leaving
you can
Run for life
Run to a life
Run get a life
Or stop

don't move
do nothing
hold your breath and hope
You better run nigger run
You better run nigger run
You better run nigger

I SHOULD HAVE ASKED BEFORE I BOUGHT YOU A JUMPER

before leaping in
I should have remembered that liberal saying
'all black people are the same'
some whiteman said that
i expect he was famous
or at least i should have known this one
we Black people all think the same
yet thinking feeling living... are specific
and specifics make the difference
blinded by love was that a hit single
I leapt not without thinking
but clutching my heart like a bloody offering to the fate devil
did i miss your prime target
ennobling skin tones
i could be your Sistah
blood ties and blood lines
make the sameness... different
where doesn't it hurt

life should not be a fight for survival
but full of diversities of good and bad
everything is linked to history
but tomorrow can't make it on yesterday
and worrying will dig furrows in your brow
and swell the sweet fullness of your lips
so that even they will taste bitter
and our palates are so full of shit already
where doesn't it hurt

you are not bad
we are not always sad
you are not a mad case
every fucker's a bit crazy
and every white man more dangerous than the maddest nigger
and this nigger is crazy
this nigger is crazy
this nigger is crazy
it's quaint to be in England
the tea is quaint
the crumpet quaint
the racism so bloody polite it's like slicing a knife through butter
i have never heard a gun shot
where doesn't it hurt

we all need a safe place
even within enemy lines
so that the 'hood becomes a blanket
let it wrap you up
let it keep you warm
you'll never really be safe
where doesn't it hurt

never trust anyone but your mother
i'm holding my hand out
but it is so dark here
can you see Black on Black
they are not the same
you
me
let's celebrate the difference
so we can nurse the pain
does it hurt

here   head
here   eyes
here   mouth
here   heart
love will do that
fill everything with anxiety
i'm sorry i should have asked before i bought you a jumper
or is it sweater in America
but lying in your arms
the pain eases
and i forget i we are 2 niggers
and nothing can really rub it better
and only a really insane fucker would want to rub out the
    Black
it is what makes us beautiful
you are beautiful

I SPEAK IN THE VOICE OF A MAN WHO HAS DIED

This is a sad voice
vibrant voice
a joyous voice
righteous voice
an indignant voice
a damaged voice
assassin's voice
a pained voice
and violent voice
a suffering voice
yet singing voice
angelic voice
and depressed voice
a poetic voice
oppressed voice
a choking voice
polluted voice
a stringent voice
victorious voice
a punished voice
ecstatic voice
a murderous voice
celebratory voice
a violated voice
yet motivated voice
a child's voice
a son's voice
a father's voice
a man's voice
a Black voice

a slave's voice
a dead voice
a free voice
free at last
free at last
free at last dead
free at last dead
my brother voice
free at last dead

TANFASTIC

I tan naturally I do
It has a lot to do with my complexion and the food I eat too
I feel sorry for the body that turns a blister red
Skin peel and burning is never my dread
And those that lie for hours leaving the beach white
They really have my sympathy for their plight
Now I begin early I go to the local gym
Two hours' aerobics, massage and a swim
Then I pop upon the sunbed for a swift half hour
this stimulates the melanin glands
Whilst increasing their reactive power
The idea is to take it slowly through the winter chills
So by springtime I emerge a dusky exotic hue

It allows me to be more colourful in my clothes
and I know you won't believe it but my dancing improves loads
By summer I am an amazing chocolate brown,
my teeth are white my eyes are bright
I dazzle when I smile
There are a few problems more mind over body
like the desire to wear less clothes and sleep with anybody

You'd be amazed at the energy that come at night by 2am
I'm Bluesing[47] with my Ganja well alight.
In the morning I sleep late seem the natural thing to do
Ah lose my job because I'm surly
but I got lots of friends in the dole queue

I have problems shopping
all the de dam assistants watching me

Mi get so angry with their suspicion
Mi shoplift for de devilry
Eventually I'm nicked de police are really crude.
Yuh should hear the names they call mi
even pigs aint that rude
One of dem hit mi
another start getting rough
when one start getting frisky mi slap him
mi had enough
Dey give mi 13 months detention
for stealing a £2.99 top
de judge si he being lenient
but mi criminal behaviour has to stop.
Dey refuse to feed mi vegetables
there's pork every time we eat
Dey make mi clean de toilets
and mi privileges are removed each week

Lawd the winter was a cold one
de sun left the sky
and slowly but surely my tan kissed me goodbye.

One day I was brown and beautiful
the next pasty and pale
The wardens give me looks of pity
and urge me to appeal
So I am free now at liberty to do as I like
so I feel it is my duty to warn others only to use quick tan
Surely it's better to be orange and disgusting
then end up like a nigger in the can.

PASSING

My name is Eloise Browning.
There is no relationship.
Neither is there anything
creative or poetic about my story. –

I am twenty-six years of age.
I understand that people say I am beautiful,
My husband tells me I am handsome.
His handsome Lily,
That's what he calls me.
Lily being sort of a pet name,
A family joke.
My grandmother tells me
That I carry the devil in my back pocket.
Due the number of risks I take.
I love taking risks.

We live in a Brownstone four storey.
And are to all intents and purposes,
Middle class. To all intents and purposes that is –
But our people they came from the land,

I have two beautiful children.
Betsy the youngest is like her father,
With eyes so dark you'd swear they were black,
If that was possible. And it sure ain't possible,
Not in this family least ways. –

I occupy myself like most married ladies,
Shopping. –
I consider shopping to be a professional occupation,

And therefore one must dress appropriately.
I like to choose loose fitting garments,
In sombre shades.

I never ever stoop
To what we refer to as nigger dressing –
You know, bright and loud.
Shoes are also very important.
Low heels and very, very comfortable.

I adore shopping, browsing round those stores –
Is my favourite occupation and –
It can be very thirsty business,
So when the need takes me
I pop into one of those little hotels
For a cup of delicious ice tea.

I love the service you get in hotels. –
Yes Ma'am; thank you Ma'am; Can I help you Ma'am?
And I must confess, though I know I shouldn't,
That my face is recognised –
In more than one
Of the more upper class established.

On this particular day,
I had been by the Five and Dime,
Do you know it by the market place?
When suddenly I had this God Almighty thirst.
I popped into this small diner.
The waitress had barely served me,
Put the drink before me,
When suddenly I could hear this silence. –
I confess I was feared,
For I have often seen the flicker of recognition
Whilst sniggering at ignorance.

I didn't want to look up
But I knew I must.
And when I did
I was shocked to see
Six coloured people at the counter.
I had heard of such things
In other parts of the Southern States.
But not in this county, here it is known
That Negroes are happy people, –
Who know their place.

I must have started praying almost at once.
Praying with a zest I never have in church on Sundays.
I prayed, make them go.
Make them go.
Dear God they must go.
But they did not move.
They did not move.

The bartender had started shouting at them and all.
And you might have thought him brave –
Considering the size and proportion.
Of two of those coloured boys.
But he had the full
And willing support of all the men in that diner.
One, even took the time out
To apologise.
– You know, for the coloured folk being there.

One was only a girl.
And the man who was picking on her
Held his face so close,
You would have sworn
That his lips were caressing her cheeks.
But she did not flinch,

She did not flinch.
Nor did she move
When he picked up the ketchup and poured it over her head.
Then, lacing his fingers in her hair.
He pulled her back
And slapped her in the face.
That was the signal for hell.

All six fell to the floor to be beaten.
– One of those coloured boys,
Try to escape over the top of the counter.
But he was pulled back,
By the teeth of a dog, in his kneecap.
So they were kicked and beaten
Till blood and ketchup became one.

Eventually, the Sheriff arrived with his deputies.
Which meant
That the use of their batons
Saved the men,
From bruising their knuckles and all. –
Till eventually all six
Were beaten right out of that diner.

More ice tea Ma'am?
The waitress's voice was like a surge of electricity
Bringing me back to fantasy.
No, thank you my bill.
I tried to control myself.
Picked up my purse
And laid my money down.

As I reached the door,
She called me again.
Excuse me Ma'am.

Ah-hah? This is a ten-dollar bill! Ah-hah.
Well thank you Ma'am
Do have a nice day. –

When I turned again
I saw that my hand had to come to rest
Next to something,
That at first was indistinguishable.
To my eye.
Then I recognised the ribbon,
From the young, coloured girl.
Still tied round strands of her hair.
Still attached to pieces of her scalp. –
Was then I knew.
Was then I knew.

So I turned.
And drawing on all the courage I could muster.
I spoke to all the people in that diner.
And I said,
What you have witnessed here today,
Is not merely the struggle for Civil Rights.
The rights that Black people have earned,
Through slavery. –
What you have witnessed here today,
Is the struggle for human rights.
The right to be recognised as equal.
In this race,
That we have called mankind.
And after what I have witnessed here today.
I, Eloise Browning.
Would never again,
Stoop to pass for white. –

REVELATIONS

I want to go to another place
where my face
strikes no wonder
walking is easy
relaxed
attitude only a state of mind
no threat to strangers
I do not know
you
why can I be so dangerous
passing on by
and wait a too long second
and home and hearth alarms whirl
loud
is my voice
even when I do not speak
but see the tinge red
on white white
hear
silence the threat
do not move here
in this place
all vacancies are full
my money equals drugs
or laid down
for a quick five pound
blow
of ecstasy
and how do I know
so much
with my head bowed

six million times
did you hear the count
did you hear the count
did you hear
capital punishment
is not a cell in
Strangeways
but a history
that lines my belly
and causes nausea to vomit over
in a venom of hatred
that sickens only me on bad days
on good days
I move easily
and smile at my men
all of them
indigo blue
mahogany brown
high yella
Black
equals not depression
but a strong belief in survival
and life is what I'm after
with highs and lows
and moans of hips on hip bone
not the quick grind
of thin-walled neighbours
but the long pause
that begs for more
give me more of you
all of you
lay here
let my thighs bind you
and rub my lips

and kiss these lips labelled ugly
and let me not suspect
that dawn brings showers
sunshine is only my father's memory
in this land
where he shivers from fear
made worse by cold
hatred is an enemy
that has no seasons
and though I try
to be brave
with chips of granite
I am weary of explaining
what is
and it is
you knew it before the word was spoken
over hot tea
in a friendly atmosphere
that places me
outside your living
an alien
you entertain
for entertainment
and I must restrain
killing you on the spot
for you meant no offence
in telling me
how you envy my not needing holidays
needing to escape
how lucky I am
being golden brown
and not black like a nigger
here comes that word
in my head it grows bigger

bigger
and how I wish
and how I wish
and how I
get up in the morning
surprises me
that I sleep
without dreaming
for escape is a space
from reality
that I seek
and I'm not angry
I'm not angry
I'm not
angry
and I'm not shouting
I'm crying
I'm crying
crying
Because I'm smiling
smiling
and it's another day
it's another day
it's another

CONTEMPT

How many tomorrows will it take?
How many tomorrows?
There is space –
Was and always has been
Space that greed cannot consume
Men cannot breed or control the world
Everyday is a disaster
In tens, hundreds, thousands.
How many tomorrows?
Contempt –
Throw it out discard it.
Put it down,
Oppress it,
Oppress it. Oppression is contempt.
And how I hate rudeness –
Change dropped from a height,
A blank stare.
The 'Lets-pretend-we-can't-understand-what-your-saying'
Ignorance.
'Are they all as Black as you?'
'Does it wash off?'
'Is it like this where you come from?'
'Bet you like the heat?'
English summers.
Racist Comedians.
Politricks.
Immigration control.
Ethnic labelling.
Poll tax.
The Census.
Equal opportunities policies.
Positive discrimination.

Tokenism.
Sexism.
Nationalism.
The National Front.
Dick heads.
Soap fans.
Disguised hatred.
Norman Tebbit.
The English Cricket team.
Football hooligans.
Bombastic councillors.
Thatcherites.
The Right
The Major-minority.
Propaganda.
Ballot fixing.
Election lies.
Guilt ridden liberals.
Fur coats.
Social Conscience.
Museums.
History.
Conquerors.
Wife beaters.
Forced entry.
Rape.
Greasy men.
Pimps.
Exposure.
The Sun.
Pornography.
Page 3.
Voyeurs.
DHSS snoopers.

Liars.
Police enquiries.
Liars.
Bible Bashers.
Missionaries.
Kinky sex.
Bondage.
Handcuffs.
Physical restraint.
Chastisement.
Child molesters.
Gay Bashers.
Cruelty to animals.
Fear of the unknown.
The National Front
Bad dreams.
The National Front.
Bloody reality.
The National Front.
Loneliness.
Failure.
Homelessness.
Growing up.
Death of my mother.
How many tomorrows will it take for peace without discrimination?
For respect without a price?
For love without the fear of hatred?
For people, for people,
for women who love women and women who love men and men who love men
for Black people for white people
For all of us.
This is all I have to say.

PLAYING FOR LIFE

Am I an actress you're fooling?
Ask me if I'm Black
Ask me that go on, ask me that.
The role I play wasn't written just for me
The script is etched upon my heart
With birth of life, I learnt my part.

The stage I play is all the world
With backdrops painted shades of white
Is how I'm seen and heard.

Upstage I play adversity
Downstage I act humility
Stage left perform soliloquy
Stage right, hear the freedom in my delivery.

Sometimes the audience the 'I' cannot see
As backstage my voice speaks distance hauntingly
And in their seats the quivering mass
Pray for the guilt-ridden scene not to last.

In mime I'm brilliant
See the emotion in my eyes
The silence is terrifying,
For in silence there are no lies.

Sometimes I do comedy
Yes, come laugh at me
Laugh, until your tears flow
Laugh, enjoy my show

Do I sing? Honey, I can hit a note
Soulful melodious so rich in the Blues
Your heart will choke.
And you've seen me dance
Seen me flick and twist
There's a rhythm in my feet
Upon which you insist

The actress has many faces,
There are many sides to me
And you will be mesmerised,
In your search for my reality

In centre stage I am the star
And the depth of my talent has taken me far
For this play I am in, is over 500 years old
The end is not yet written,
The final chapter still untold
And when it is
Then you who have been watching
Will finally understand,
That the need for all my acting
Has been your oppression White Man

LEANING AGAINST TIME

I see myself waiting
on this street corner of all that is England
Like a prostitute tired of the business
Yet waiting still
for that special lover.

Blind –
to the big pockets of small change
and no paper for creativity –
fat wallets with no lips to shape a conversation

My eyes turned down to the dirt of my situation
and see there reflected
the passing in all shades
of this
Black and white reality.

Those too lean to lay a hip next to
Those stomachs-wider than desire
could stretch a leg over

I hear their mutterings
the cursing of
'who she think she is'
'too ugly for my taste'
'too worn'
'too wide'
'too choosy for her own good'

I hear
but like a deaf mute,

I remain as still as any public art commission
a subject of debate for some possibly,
possibly a waste of space,
life, for others
and therefore of absolutely no interest

On bad days
when chills whip past
this place I have taken for my own
I tell myself
this waiting will be the death of me
And the full glow of my living
will simply fade into that
darker shade of blood red dead

Sometimes I shuffle impatient
trying to hustle up an early arrival
but my welcoming dance
is mauled by the stubbornness of my leg(s)

My body takes on the bruising
of this waiting
as I am jostled by incidents out of my control
But I remain steadfast
And if you pass by
you will see me
A sentinel
A believer
Keeping my faith
Leaning Against Time

I BELIEVE THAT THE CONSPIRACY THEORY EXISTS

I believe that the conspiracy theory exists at all times and in all agendas. How sad am I?

I believe that every artist will break any rules to ensure the continuality of their creative flow. I believe that those who suggest that we come together to create networks regardless of race and gender and share our ideas are possibly fools but more likely incapable of formulating their own creative starting point.

I believe that every arts officer, no, I'll rephrase that to some arts officers, mainly those whose department is not mainstream, read Euro-centric, goes to work each day apprehensive as to whether their position is in jeopardy.

I believe that as Black artists we are the warriors and caretakers of our mutual cultures and heritages. I do not view either you or myself as soldiers. Soldiers fight wars and once you start fighting you must always defend yourself. I do not see myself as defensive but I do see myself as maintaining a close watch on what I am, a Black woman of art.

I believe that taking people as you find them is a stupid thing to do. I am stupid. My trust is constantly abused. But without trust I will expire. My trust is running out.

I make sweeping statements. I make sweeping statements about Black people. My people. Positive statements. I make sweeping statements about white people. They are not always positive. They fall from my mouth like an invisible flow of blood spurting from a wound. I am too often wounded.

Like most artists I have lonely times. Times when the need to debate, laugh, simply let my mouth wear itself dry with talking, are so great, that despair clouds an already cloudy Manchester sky. I run up an enormous one-number international phone bill.

The floor of my mind is not scattered with discarded poems but with application forms. Begging letters for a heritance that is rightfully mine, yours, ours. Even though our hands are not scarred with labour.

My backside. This rump of Africa modified by my Liverpool mother is cramped with attending meetings that serve no purpose but to shuffle papers to keep arts officers on salary.

My hearing is aching from good intentions that have worn away my inner ear. My eyes are rubbed red with the dazzle of strategy papers, written in languages so dense that the intention to say nothing in over ten thousand words has been successfully achieved.

I believe Black to be the most powerful self-declaration we can make.

I believe that Black unites us when used by us. I believe that black (small case b) can and is used to lump us into a disgruntled mass and forces us to wrangle between ourselves. To push forward, pass one another. To make our voice heard above the grumbling of the others. It exposes our weaknesses by turning individuals into race disclaimers in order to disentangle themselves into another and what they see more exclusive identity. I see this black as ghettoised. I see it as identified with trouble and troubles. I see this black as a fundraising tool for non-black organisations. I see this black as increase in their revenue, a large project grant, and useful publicity. All the things it does not do for the Black (upper case B) organisations.

I can't see the future. I am clever but not that slick. I believe in a future, I have to, out of respect to all those who helped to put me here. Ancestors never leave you. Mothers refuse to.

I believe that our greatest asset is our stubbornness. It is our strength. It is that lip that sticks out and will not budge.

I believe that our minds are not on the verge of collapse; our spirit has not left us. I do not recognise all of us in the media. I despair but have not given up yet on those written under headlines blazoned with death, for even if they are lost to us, their children remain and if they themselves are children, their families of all ages remain. I will work with all of our people for all of our people.

I believe that art is therapeutic, whether you are involved passively or actively.

I believe that to be passive is to wrap the mind in defeat.

I believe that the simple coming together, the drawing on words, the debate vocally, the rage and the laughter, is vital for us, so that we may consider where we are and where we are going based on where we have been. For without all of these we may just start to believe all that is said about us.

A CLASSIC

Somebody farted.
I'm telling you, somebody farted.
Whilst the speaker was generalising
On gender
And cultural and social ethics
Just at that moment
When sleepers snore
And non-smokers cough and cackle
Paper crackles.
Just when you'd expect
A polite form of social interchange
Some dirty sod
Let one off.
And we,
We coughed it out of existence.
After all
Isn't that what conferences are for
A lot of hot air.

THEY TELL LIES

They tell lies
and describe images so confusing
that even they fail
to recognise the subject.
The subject being me.

They make demons out of small children laughing
too loudly, on a street corner
and harlots of young women
possibly too young for short-short skirts and bosoms blooming.
But harlots no, surely.

They fantasise of a time without us
and cannot remember when that was
and fail to comprehend how boring their lives were
and would be if we left.

They swear oaths
pressing palms white to squashed pink
calling on God to bear witness to their testament of truth
while their tongues babble like the devil.

Telling lies in my house
meant first a reprimand
no supper
early to bed
and the smarting slap of
don't do that again.

No lies were tolerated
None. Not fibs.

Not, especially, white lies.
Be true to yourself spoke my mother
And I try.
And it's hard.
Ssshhh, listen
you don't even have to strain to hear their whisperings.
Whispering, even now as I tell you again.
They're telling lies about you and me.

PRODUCED BY GYENYAME FOR PERFORMING ARTS

Original Cast 1998

Mary Seacole	Hyacinth Nicholls
Mother Seacole	Bianca Campbell
Local Man	Wills Morgan
Florence Nightingale	Caroline Leeks
William Russell	Ian Jervis
Mr.Grant / Captain / Soldier #3	Nicholas Garrett
Young Man / Soldier #2	Andrew Clarke
Sergeant / Soldier #1	Ronald Samm
Young Girl	Davina Wright
Woman 1 /3 / Nurse	Helen Gasztowt-Adams
Woman 2 / Nurse	Helen Astrid
Officer / Soldier #4	Jeremy Birchall

Cast in order of appearance

RUSSELL – William H Russell
SEACOLE – Mary Seacole
MRS GRANT
MR GRANT
LOCAL JAMAICAN
SOUTH AMERICAN GENTLEMAN
NIGHTINGALE
OFFICER

Supporting cast in order of appearance
Chorus Woman
First man
Second man
Non-singing cast
Frocked doctor taken from chorus

The Crimean

Smoky dark stage, man sits at a camp table & lights an oil lamp.
He begins typing and reads aloud as he works

RUSSELL

This is William H. Russell, Special Correspondent in the theatre of war of 1856, and we fight an enemy who knows no limits.

Indeed, he is a fool with no regard to the danger.

We do not honour him; we honour and respect only those who have joined the battle, the men at arms.

Readers, the battle is fierce, the suffering enormous, the Queen's sons are brave but not invincible.

The battlefield is awash with blood, who could not weep at the sight?

Miss Nightingale has established her hospital away from the action, it is not enough.

You, in the comfort of your homes, please give what support you can.

Linen for bandages, hand-knitted socks for warmth and your prayers to help end this devil of a war.

Battle sounds and groans getting louder until it becomes a human hum.

CHORUS

Mother help me.
Oh God, Oh God.
I don't want to die.

My leg, where is my leg?
I'm blind I can't see.

*SET – a warm glow begins in the centre of the smoke, like a fire
beginning to catch light.*

WOMAN *(Off stage)*
There my son, there.
Let this ease you
So you can sleep.

FIRST MAN
I'm so cold.
So cold.

WOMAN *(Off stage)*
Here is my hand son.
Here take my hand.

SECOND MAN
Is that you Mother,
Is that you?

*SET – SEACOLE steps into the light stage left as frocked doctor's
dash about calling out orders spoken by the chorus*

CHORUS
Bring me bandages.
Some rum.
A saw.

*SEACOLE tries to catch their attention and then facing the rising
dawn she speaks to the heavens.*

SEACOLE

I tried to volunteer.
They rejected me.
Ms Nightingale humoured me.
But still I came full steam and independent
And now like a beggar seeking alms
I try to catch their attention.
I am no beggar I am a dutiful healer
And that is what I came to do
And will do.

*SET – SEACOLE turns up stage and walks slowly into the smoke
of the battlefield calling out.*

SEACOLE

I am here my sons.
I am here

Off stage voices cry out her name

CHORUS

Mother Seacole,
Lord Bless you
Mother Seacole

RUSSELL *(Spoken)*

One woman, steadfast, determined
And independently resourced
Eases the moral, physical well being of the men.
They call her 'Yellow Woman'
But her colour matters little,
Her origins are of no interest.
Ladies and Gentlemen I
Give you the life of Mary Seacole,

DIRECTION *Sung*
Mother of our men.

Jamaica.
Interior of SEACOLE's parents' house.
The grey tones of war are replaced by the warm orange of a tropical
climate. A heavyset man approaches the table covered with a white
cloth and as he sits, he calls out to MRS GRANT his 'Wife'.

SEACOLE enters stage right sits by his feet as a child.

GRANT
Girl, girl
Can you no see me sat here?
With my belly groaning.
How many times have ah to tell ye
The way to a man's heart
Is through his belly.
A body canna love without fuel
And food is the fuel.

A smiling Black woman (MRS GRANT) carries a plate of food
across to him.
MRS GRANT brushes her hand across his head and he almost
unconsciously pushes away her gesture of tenderness to turn all his
attention to the plate before him.

GRANT
You can cook,
I give you that.
Aye and you can look after a man

After dark too,
That so you can.

He rubs his stomach satisfied and she immediately clears the table.
He stands using the white cloth as a napkin to wipe his mouth.

GRANT
Fare de well lassie I'm going home.
Fare de well lassie my orders have come.
And I know you will weep and aye you might cry
But take it from me this is goodbye.
I've nothing to leave you but memories
And hope (you) no regret your time with me
You're a Creole woman no young but your strong
So go catch ye a nigga and make him your man

The military tattoo begins to play out indicating the increasing distance of the departing army. GRANT marches on the spot facing stage left. SEACOLE moves towards him.

He throws the white cloth at her and turns stage left falling into the band's military march that has taken up the rhythm of his singing.

SEACOLE the 'child' stands takes the tablecloth and wraps it like a shawl around her head and shoulders.

SEACOLE
See how he goes steadfast and strong
A soldier and a gentleman of him I am so proud
He was my father though he never stayed
He was my father though he went away
When I am careful of money in my hand
I think of my father that sure and canny man
I am his daughter though he never knew me
I am his daughter I am sure he would be proud of me

MRS GRANT now takes up the tattoo but bringing to it the tilt of calypso. SEACOLE the 'child' hands the table cloth back to MRS GRANT and leaves stage right

MRS GRANT

So yuh pack up and leave mi
Deafh to mi cri
Yuh never tel mi yuh love mi
Mi nev'r hear dat lie
Yuh jus pack up and leave mi
Kiss the air goodbye

Kissing her lips MRS GRANT stands and turns upstage. Her body rocks to the closing notes of music as she rolls the cloth and holds it cradled in her army.

SCENE THREE

Jamaica.

Exterior of SEACOLE's parents' house

A local man enters he is clutching his stomach causing him to almost hop into the room. It is obvious he is in pain but he is also excited indicated by his gesticulating. His dress though poor also indicates his life role of a bit of a wag.

LOCAL JAMAICAN

Sistah Nurse mi need yuh bad-bad.
Mi belli bawling like it fire
An' as soon as mi stand so, mi must sit.
Feel like mi dun lost half mi stomach already
and if yuh no fix it quick,
into the latrine the whole of mi body will go.

MRS GRANT only turns her head.

MRS GRANT
Wat yuh drink?

LOCAL JAMAICAN
Rrrrrrr. Rhum
Sistah Nurse,
but don't cuss mi
De whole island is afire wiv excitement
Now de army dun gwan.
Wat dey brings nuthink.
Wat deys do nuthink.
Wat dey leaves nuthink.
Gawd save Jamaica an' dam de King.

MRS GRANT
Noh soh quick wiv yuh mouth
Some leave someting
Look here see dis

She holds out her arms that carry the cloth now rolled into baby swaddling.

LOCAL JAMAICAN
Gad Sistah Nurse
yuh gon got yuh a yellow child
Who will nurse folk?
whilst yuh breed dat

MRS GRANT
I muss give her up
But only short-short time.
Den from mi she will learn

De herbs and secrets to cure,
So stupid men like yuh
Caan ruin dire bellies
Until they run as fast as yuh mouth.

The lights dim. SEACOLE the 'child' picks up the cloth moves out of the ever-dimming lights to stage left and begins to rip the fabric into uniform lengths.

MRS GRANT lays down the cloth and turns her attention to the man.

MRS GRANT *(She repeats herself)*
I muss give her up
But only short-short time.
Den from mi she will learn
De herbs and secrets to cure,
So stuupide men like yuh
Caan ruin dire bellies
Until they run as fast as yuh mouth.

She gives him a potion and he swallows it eagerly then she turns her attention to the baby leaving stage left.

The man crawls into a small ball, centre stage front and closes his eyes to sleep.

SCENE FOUR

Jamaica.

Seconds on he rolls over, opens his eyes, stretches and yawns, patting his belly with satisfaction.

LOCAL JAMAICAN

Mi fel good an' mi promise
Nevah to fel badd aging
Mi fel good and mi promise
Nevah to fel bad again
No more rhum an' wimmin
No more rhum an' wimmin,
Lawd!
No more rhum an' wimmin

He rubs his head looking puzzled

But I is a man who does need to take
A lickle rhum fi mi old health sake
For mi back it do ache
And mi bones dey do creak
And without any rhum
mi go dizzy and weak
But if de brew be badd
Den mi belli explode
So no
No more rhum an' wimmin
Lawd
No more rhum an' wimmin

He nods his head trying to convince himself.

Mi a simple mhan and mi needs are de same
Fi de odd night mi need a woman to lay
At mi side to ease de pain of de life
So I should get mi a wife but den she a breed
An' make more mouth fi mi to feed
Dey will demand more an' more
An' den no more rhum for sure

Lawd no more rhum for sure

MRS GRANT returns stage left.

LOCAL JAMAICAN
Dere a fine woman over der
See de skill she has to nurse and care
From simple herb she mix an' boil
She do stop mi belli painful roar
Maybe someting she could Obeah
To stop mi belli play bad on mi
Den I'll still have rhum an' wimmin
Lawd
I'll still hav rhum an' wimmin

The man performs a little dance it is almost lewd then suddenly he grabs his stomach with one hand, with the other obviously grabs his bottom, and runs exiting stage right.

SCENE FIVE

Jamaica.

Exterior SEACOLE's parents' house. MRS GRANT is intent on mixing brews, periodically she halts to peek at the baby, whisper to it and kiss it.

Orchestra plays intro bars of 'Yellow Bird' before MRS GRANT starts to sing:

MRS GRANT
Yellow Bird up high in banana tree
Yellow bird yuh sit all alone like me

Did your lady frien'
Leave de nest again
Dat is very sad
Make yuh feel so bad
Yuh can fly away
In the sky away
Yuh more lucky dan mi.

MRS GRANT laughs to herself, takes up the child tucking it into the bone of her hip and binding it there with cloth so her hands are free to continue her work.

SEACOLE who has been watching everything from the sidelines now moves closer so that she can see exactly what MRS GRANT is mixing.

MRS GRANT
Take dis herb and mix just soh
Watch mi Mary Jane
For dis is de best schooling
Yuh will hever get
Jamaicans are proud
But de world she is cruel
Even to ah baby as yella as yuh
If yuh life to prosper
To make it better dan dis
Take heed of wat I teach
For over der place
Where travel yuh go
The Obeah skill is de best to know.

SEACOLE sings in reply directly to her mother.

SEACOLE

That's how your doctrine became mine
I listened, watched
The herbs you prepared
The poultice you blended
As people gathered for your cures
I too took my patients
First the doll, silent to my care
Then cat, dog or a lizard I might catch
Practice over error to reach perfect
And make ready in 1850 for that whore
Cholera
Men fell of all classes
Jamaican Natives, Creole, and Black
And my precious 97th infantry
They had surgeon skills but some things they lacked
So I gathered your herbs together
Knowing soon there'd come the call
To doctrine officers and lower ranks of men
To banish out that she devil
And restore their constitutions good again
Your spirit burns anew in me
So I am at pains to nurse all suffers
And banish their misery

SCENE SIX

South America.

A local South American man walks across the stage carrying a small bundle.

He begins to chant 'Cholera' a cappella then he starts to hum at a higher pitch:

SOUTH AMERICAN
Cholera is a killer
Cholera will take them all
Take your mother and your sister
Kill a baby barely born
Cholera is a killer
Kill a child that's part way grown
Take your father
Take a brother
Cholera will take them all.

SEACOLE
Give me the child that you carry
before you lay it in its grave
If I might see death's first face of glory
I might discover how to stop the killer plague

SOUTH AMERICAN
Will you cut it?

SEACOLE
I must cut it
But think how many I might then save

SOUTH AMERICAN
This is a child

SEACOLE
No.
No, it's just a body
And for life
Sacrifices must be made.

SEACOLE turns away cradling the child's corpse in her arms then she lays it on the ground and kneels beside it.

SEACOLE
Soft skin
Soft skin
Is it right
what I'm doing?
It must be right
What I'm doing
Hold the blade steady
Then cut, snip, pull back the skin
This heart small,
In death so swollen
Cut, snip, pull back the skin
I see yellow to the core
Poisonous infliction on rich and poor
Like a rat spreading vermin
Like a hunter trapping prey
Here in this baby I see the ruin
Now cholera you will pay
Stitch. Stitch. Stitch. Stitch.
Small and dainty.
For this child I stitch

SOUTH AMERICAN
Is it is done?

SEACOLE bows her head and then turns her face towards the sky before reaching down to pick up the corpse and hand it back to the South American man.

SEACOLE
It's over for him
My need is done
I will never wash away his memory
As so easily, I will wash away his blood
Take him now to a place restful

Take him and bury him as though a prince
He has been a martyr to my learning
And to the whole of medicine
I have no cure but better understanding
And some day of cholera we will be rid.

She wipes her hand on the now bloody white cloth. A gentleman appears wearing a monocle, which he uses to peer closely at the sight. In his left hand he holds a walking cane, which he uses to address SEACOLE.

GENTLEMAN
Good God woman, what is this savagery?

SEACOLE
I believe it is called an autopsy

GENTLEMAN
You would cut a child M'arm.

SEACOLE
It is dead sir,
I do it no harm
I only wish to see an end
to the pestilence of
Cholera,
cholera, cholera.

The stage pitches into darkness.

The Crimean and London, England.

RUSSELL is sat at his desk typing, the desk lamp is the only lighting on stage.

There are 4 or 5 chairs in a line to indicate a waiting queue of women to be recruited by NIGHTINGALE.

RUSSELL *(Spoken)*
14th November 1854. Post battle conditions at Balaclava and Inkermann are almost too demonic to tell. Those men injured by the vile Russians now lie awaiting death by the shipload, heading to the hospitals at Scutari where their only hope is a quick passing from this life to the next. The injured are so many that hands cannot begin to tend their needs. '*I was sick and ye, visited me*'. But who will visit these shores where the death sits upon the shoulder of those who can barely breathe life into each new day.

The stage is fully lit to indicate the scene has now shifted to England. Three uniformed men are milling about.

NIGHTINGALE enters stage left and walks down stage. She is agitated, appearing to start walking about, but she remains on the one spot.

NIGHTINGALE
They must be clean
They must be sober
They must be dedicated women to the task
No fat dames of fourteen stones or over
The provision of bedsteads is not strong enough.

For fifty thousand soldiers
I too need an army
Of women capable of care
To nurse the wounded
Not weep for the dying
For weeping is a weakness
I will not bear.

NIGHTINGALE takes the seat RUSSELL has vacated at the table.

SEACOLE enters stage right, walking upstage left turning towards NIGHTINGALE.

SEACOLE
And visit I did.
Eager and naive
Carrying upon my person testimony of my skill
Her peculiar fitness, in a constitutional point of view,
For medical attendant, need no comment.
And so I was received in silence
With eyes full of astonishment.
That my skin should surprise them
Was only as I had expected
Not black as Negro but brown and not dark
But surely not a sight to shock.
Some never even saw this one who in time to come
Would carry with pride the name Mother
Crimean heroine
Yellow Woman.

SEACOLE sits on one of the row of chairs and makes as to write a letter.

SEACOLE
Dear Secretary-at-War
I write to offer my skills in medicine
What I am apt to call doctrine
There are many who can pledge to my ability
Please find enclosed a few of their testimonies

One of the uniformed men rips a letter into small piece tossing the paper into the air.

SEACOLE
What time I wasted on the postal services
What intelligence I lacked for I never realised that
My letters were directed to the bin.

NIGHTINGALE
Fourteen women rallied to the call.
Fourteen volunteers,
Good God Why isn't there more.

NIGHTINGALE gathers her papers together still in an agitated manner and leaves the stage.

SEACOLE
Remembering the stamina of my Scottish father
I never wavered from my goal
That the Secretary-at-war might ignore me
Failed to deter me
So to the Quartermaster-General I made to implore.

SEACOLE again sits to write

SEACOLE
Dear Quartermaster-General
I write to offer my skills in medicine

What I am apt to call doctrine
There are many who can pledge to my ability
Please find enclosed a few of their testimonies

Whilst SEACOLE has been writing an officer has arrived on stage
moving the table to stage right he sits and begins to open and then
discard letters. His action with one in particular is deliberate. He
listens with his head to one side and a barely hidden grin on his
face. When SEACOLE has finished he stands and with his hands
clasped behind him addresses her directly:

OFFICER
You want to go to war madam.
Are you sure madam?
This is the army madam.
We do not recruit women

SEACOLE walks to indicate a distance travelled finally sitting
again on the row of chairs. Her back is very straight.

NIGHTINGALE pushes the officer to one side and takes his place
at the table, which is now centre stage. She is singing while as she
settles herself.

OFFICER
You want to go to war madam.
Are you sure madam?
This is the army madam.
We do not recruit women

NIGHTINGALE
We have to do what we need to do
For war has its own demands
We need to care for every man
do the best we can

And my standards are always English
as lady I'll always be
Any tardy and sluttish behaviour
will have to deal with me
Cleanliness, I demand only cleanliness
I want no heathen practices on my wards
Ban all the natives
They only come to steal
If they are local to the land
They are not wanted here
It's English soldiers we heal
It's only English soldiers we'll heal
So we are set to do what we need to do
for war makes its own demands
And I offer a balaclava of comfort
for every wounded man
We came to save the English
Only the English soldier
It's what my birthright commands
I light my lamp to guide the way
For the wounded English man.

NIGHTINGALE rises and walks upstage right gazing into the distance. She speaks to herself.

NIGHTINGALE
If my arithmetic does not fail me.
This is a bloody equation indeed,
Twenty thousand soldiers wounded
and I have only thirty-eight nursing trainees.

NIGHTINGALE returns to the desk resting her chin in the palm of one hand. SEACOLE rises and slowly walks towards her to lightly touch her on the shoulder saying:

SEACOLE *(Spoken)*
Miss Nightingale.
You seemed to be daydreaming

NIGHTINGALE's posture is immediately rigid and composed.

NIGHTINGALE *(Spoken)*
I can ensure you madam that wasn't the case.
Have we been introduced?
What you see here, are all the horrors,
The scavenges of war.
Men are dying;
I have no time for social entertaining.
Madam,
Is there anything more?

SEACOLE
From you, oh no.
From you, oh no.
I do not berate you;
For in truth I do respect you
But I wonder what you see
When you see the colour of me.
Healing is not your monopoly
Like death, it is a human reality.
You need not dismiss me
I am free like you to go
But do not be fooled
By this retiring
For it is to the battlefront I go.

NIGHTINGALE
Madam I choose to ignore your insolence
For you say you need a place to sleep
The laundry in there

Is a woman who space for you will make.
I have no time for petty quarrelling
I know my place
I suggest that you learn yours
For though a nurse
I am still a lady
And on that,
I choose to end this discourse.

NIGHTINGALE walks towards SEACOLE pausing for a moment then sweeps past her with a flourish of her skirts to talk with one of the uniformed men. He acknowledges her with a salute. He then obviously turns his back to SEACOLE giving his full attention to the clipboard in his hand.

OFFICER
Officer Cromby,
Lieutenant Smyth,
Lady Bartholomew,
Miss Price,
Elizabeth Henry,
First Sergeant York,
Servant girl Mary,
Common maid Ann,
Mrs Henry Norman.
Sorry we have taken all we can.
Anyone who is still waiting
You may leave
Wait no more.
The Quartermaster thanks you for your intention
But we have enough for this war

Laughter follows his announcement, he now looks directly at SEACOLE.

OFFICER
Madam!

SEACOLE
Sir!

OFFICER
You want to go to war madam.
Are you sure madam?
This is the army madam.
We do not recruit women

OFFICER marches off, his laughter is audible.

SCENE EIGHT

Dockside.

SEACOLE is sat on a trunk looking dishevelled.

SEACOLE
Then I shall sail by any means
I would walk t'is sorrow I cannot fly
But I will arrive there by and by
I am not defeated by rejection
It serves to heighten my determination
Of this one thing I am sure

SEACOLE stands and storms forward to centre stage then back to the table turns and bangs her fist on it.

SEACOLE
Damn the Englishman
Damn the Englishman
Who do they think they are?
See how the look at me
Am I such a sight to see?
I am a Jamaican born free
These hands can cure illness
These lands have yet to see
This mind can make remedy
Their doctors will beg know from me
Damn the Englishman
Damn the Englishman
As they turn from me
My sweet men of 97th and 48th infantry
Defend England's territory.
I'm pledged to nurse the ailing
To doctrine any who have need of me
This is my fate and my destiny
Damn the Englishman
Damn the Englishman
Damn the Englishman
Damn the Englishman

Loud crashing sound like cannon fire the stage is blacked out.

CAST in order of appearance:
Four Paperboys
William H. Russell Captain
Soldier
Four Footmen.
First Woman & Second Woman (The 'Gossiping women')
Cluster of Women.
Mary Seacole
The Duppies
Soldier One
Soldier Two
Soldier Three
Group of soldiers
Third Woman
Soldier Four
Soldier Five
Soldier Six
Soldier Seven (Captain Peel)
Monsieur Jullien
Wild African Woman
Nurse One
Nurse Two
Young Man
Boy
Jamaican Girl
Supporting singing cast in order of appearance
Woman
First man
Second man
Choir

SCENE ONE

Crimea and London.

As the audience returns to their seats, sat at each theatre entrance is a young ragamuffin hawking newspapers. They ignore the women and reject the men who cannot proffer a farthing in order to buy.

On stage with their back to the audience stand a Captain and regular soldier, there smoke is settling in front (far back) of them.

RUSSELL is madly typing at his desk.

PAPERBOYS
Only a farthing sir,
Only a farthing.
Get your paper Sir
Only a farthing.
The Turks are defeated sir
And the Russians are running,
Read about the Crimean victory sir,
Only a farthing.

They hold up their sheets for the audience to see as they walk through the theatre towards and over the stage they speak.

FIRST PAPERBOY *(Spoken)*
We'd be better off boy outside
There they 'ave a better class of audience.

SECOND PAPERBOY shoves another boy, he staggers backwards as he recovers he starts to dance a jig, and the others begin to sing.

PAPERBOYS

Old King Cole was a merry old soul
And a merry old soul was he
He called for his pot and he called for pipe
And he called for his fiddlers three
The Russians are dead and the Crimean is red
From the soldiers who paid the price
For daring to anger the English might
We flattened them just like lice.

PAPERBOYS jump about then stamp their feet four times before running form the stage.

RUSSELL begins to hum and speak the original version of King Cole, allowing the change of tempo to register.

SCENE TWO

Crimea.

RUSSELL is walking slowly singing the Punch version of the song.

RUSSELL

Dame Seacole was a kindly old soul
And a kindly old soul was she
You might call for your pot,
you might call for your pipe
In her tent on 'the Col' so free
That berry-brown face,
with a kind heart's trace
Impressed in each wrinkle sly,
Was a sight to behold,

through the snow-clouds rolled
Across the iron sky.

Two SOLDIERS stand facing up stage left their backs toward the
CAPTAIN.

CAPTAIN *(Speaking)*
You may stand at ease soldier

SOLDIERs *(Speaking)*
Thank you sir.

Moving exactly together the SOLDIERS stand at ease, their
hands clasped behind their backs palms towards the audience.

CAPTAIN *(he turns as he sings)*
Another war another memoir,
Another memory to take home to England.
How company will rally
To hear of my escapades
And the stories I have
Are wondrous, gallant,
Valiant and victorious.
And you soldier
What memory do you have?

SOLDIER *(he now turns to face down stage)*
Captain may I make my report on all that I have see
I swear to God I have never seen before the sight that
met my eyes
For amongst the fallen and wounded as gentle as an angel
I came across the one they call the yellow woman
I heard her speak to the injured
In a voice so full of love

And those who are not destined to return
Through cloud of death before they died
Clasped her hand and called her mother
They called her mother
And not breaking hearts, she replied yes, my son.

CAPTAIN
A woman you say

SOLDIER
Yes Sir

CAPTAIN
Not Nightingale you say

SOLDIER
No Sir

CAPTAIN
By heavens
We will have to make sure
She is mentioned in dispatches
We have to make sure
She receives due respect
That this woman isn't forgotten
Seacole you say
A native you say
A Jamaican
Well war has its surprises
And Nightingale still busy
But protected in her hospital
Women!
I'll never understand them

RUSSELL *(starts singing Old King Cole again)*
Still she'd take her stand, as blithe and bland
With her stores and jolly old soul
And – be the right man in the right place who can
The right woman was Dame Seacole.
And now the good soul is 'in the hole'
What red coat in all the land
But to set her upon her legs again
Will not lend a willing hand.

RUSSELL stands pushing his chair determinedly away and with a flourish pulls the paper from the typewriter and reads:

In every bush and on every yard of blood- stained ground lay a dead or dying Russian. The well-known bearskins of our Guards, the red coats of our Infantry, and the bright blue of the French Chasseurs, revealing each a silent horror in the glades, and marking the spot where stark and stiff a corpse lay contorted on the grass, pointed out the scenes of the bloodiest contests. The dead were happy, the dull, cold eye, the tranquil brow, the gently opening lips, which had given escape to the parting spirit as it fled from its bleeding shell, showed how peacefully a man may die in battle, pierced by the rifle ball. The British and the French, many of whom had been murdered by the Russians as they lay wounded, wore terrible frowns on their faces, with which the agonies of death had clad them. Some in their last throes had torn up the earth in their hands, and held the grass between their fingers up towards heaven.

Surrey Gardens, London.

A map of Surrey Gardens projected on backdrop

*FOUR FOOTMEN walk from the back of the theatre to the stage.
They hold candelabra aloft singing in slow acapella. As they begin
singing, the full cast begin to take the stage in groups.*

FOUR FOOTMEN
Surrey Gardens welcomes the Mary Seacole Fund
And her patrons wish the best to everyone.
By the pledge they have taken
To solicit funds
By this auspicious occasion
And improve her lot
Her majesty the Queen
In gratitude for the lady's work
For the navy
For the army
For the British nation's men
Does acknowledge this service
With concern for the lady's welfare.
And so says His Royal Highnesses T
he Prince of Wales
The Duke of Cambridge
And the Duke of Edinburgh.
As her patrons.

Two gossiping women.

*The women cluster together like hens moving their necks to see as
much a possible without turning their bodies.*

FIRST WOMAN
Have you,
have you,
have you,
Have you seen her

SECOND WOMAN
Have you,
have you,
have you,
Have you seen her

FIRST WOMAN
My dear
My dear
My dear
One thousand tickets

SECOND WOMAN
My dear
My dear
My dear
One thousand tickets

FIRST WOMAN
Ten thousand tickets
And the woman is Black

SECOND WOMAN
What do you mean she is Black,
Like in coloured
Or in Black!

FIRST WOMAN
Coloured. Black.
Coloured. Black.
What does it matter
She's a coloured

SECOND WOMAN
Oh, it matters.
Indeed, it matters.
My son called her mother.
What shame and scandal
To have a coloured mother.

The two women scatter whispering and are joined by more women.

CLUSTER OF WOMEN
What shame and scandal
To have a coloured mother.
What shame and scandal
To have a coloured mother

RUSSELL enters waving his arms grandly. He sings an extract of the same lyrics from Act One Scene One.

RUSSELL
They call her 'Yellow Woman'
But her colour matters little,
Her origins are of no interest.
Ladies and Gentlemen
I give you Mary Seacole,
Mother of our men.
Mother of our men.

*SEACOLE is in a bath chair and wheeled on stage left
RUSSELL fusses about her.*

RUSSELL
I hope you are comfortable

SEACOLE
I could not be better
I'm ill but not frail
I'm sick but yet I'm strong
And for all who have come
To honour me this night
I shall yet stand
Indeed I'll walk
I think I'll dance.

*The orchestra plays a reggae beat in andante that changes into a
slow waltz as at its crescendo the tempo changes to an 'Alla Marcia'.*

SEACOLE and RUSSELL dance together for under a minute.

*While this is going on the bath chair is removed and replaced with
an old armchair.*

*SEACOLE staggers as though to faint and RUSSELL quickly
assists her into sitting down.*

*The marching tempo is now played at a hushed volume as one-by-
one members of the cast walk past SEACOLE.*

*SEACOLE raises her hand towards each face and they grasp it
and bow or courtesy their respect.*

SEACOLE repeats to each of them.

SEACOLE
I remember you,
I remember

Once again the orchestra plays the first note of a waltz but SEACOLE raises her hand to stop them and rising walks downstage until she reaches the edge and looks upwards towards the heavens.

SEACOLE *(Spoken)*
Wait don't close the door.
Let the duppy come
Let the duppy come
Let the duppy come
All my boys are welcomed here
Let the duppy come.

The stage and auditorium fall silent as the lights of the full house are dimmed to almost blackout.

THE DUPPIES
From boy to man
I wanted to go to war
To take my stand
For the rights of an English man
All my comrades were as loyal as I
Willing to fight
Though not eager to die
Then on the morning of the battle cry
They died.
They died.
Do you remember the roar of the cannon
The crack of the gun
The sniper's gun

The screeching shredding of skin
The wet explosion of a beating heart
Then the earth-shattering silence
As they died
As they died
They died.

Immediately as SEACOLE turns, the lights flash up.

SCENE FOUR

Surrey Gardens, London.

A woman's laughter peals out, glasses clink and there is the hum of happy voices.

Soldiers are stood about in groups of 1 x 2, 1 x 3, and 1 x 6.

SOLDIER ONE
The first time I saw her for the first time
Before the smoke of battle had lifted from the air
Who would have thought a woman
Especially of her creed and colour
Would want to come to the aid of the British soldier

SOLDIER TWO
The first time I saw her for the first time
As I came to consciousness
In the bosom of her arms
I know that it sounds ridiculous
But I thought that she was my mother
That was the confusion from the pain

A third soldier walks towards the first two mimicking the action of the Local Jamaican from the first act.

SOLDIER THREE
I couldn't stand I couldn't sit
But I could squat
Lord,
Did I squat.
Oh, my belly was so heavy
Swollen like a mother near her time
I like my prog but as soon as I swallowed

He groans bends double and makes as though to dash across the room.

Make room.
Make room.

The soldiers scatter in repulsion to let him pass

ALL SOLDIERS
There's a man in need
There's a man in need
Make room
Make room

SOLDIER THREE *(pulls himself up in recovery loudly sighing his relief.*
You can laugh
But let me tell you
Whatever she gave me worked.

The full cast meander around the stage. Three women stand upstage left pointing, laughing and applauding as though they are watching something.

THIRD WOMAN *(singing directly to a soldier)*
Your letters brought joy to our mother's heart
Though your affection it seemed was confused
For you called a woman we had never met
Mother too.
For God's will we had prayed for you
For his blessing to keep you alive
But I know understand it was Seacole's hand
That turned the healing tide.

SOLDIER FOUR *(mimes horse riding he crosses the stage and stops near SEACOLE)*
Lie down mother,
Mother lie down
Don't you hear that the guns are firing
You take risks mother
That you should not mother
What is the use of you dying
See the men in the trench over there
Hear their pathetic cries
Who will nurse them
Who will nurse them
If you allow yourself to die
So lie down mother
Mother lie down
For today let the snipers cry.

The company laugh into their drinks.

CAPTAIN
Many of the ordinary men
The lower ranks I'm sure you understand
Were nervous of going to hospital
They objected to the last man
But it was nourishment they yearned for

A little chicken broth can be a mighty cure
To what ails a soldier-at-war and keeps him fighting
She had the skill of a master chef
Like a magician she conjure a dish
That would keep an army marching
And make a gentleman enlist.

SOLDIER FIVE *(holds his hands high as though he is telling a
fisherman's 'big catch' whopper story)*
They were this big I tell you
I had jammed them at Frenchman's Hill
Three doctors had looked at them
One two three
One two three
And not one had a cure for me
So down the hill I did go
To put my faith in Mother Seacole.

SOLDIER SIX *(to the original cholera tune)*
Cholera took my body
Like with poison I was sick
And I thought my life was over
As cholera took its grip

Music moves accelerando.

SOLDIER SIX
I don't know what she gave me
I never heard her say it would cure
But as I swear here…

He raises his arm to a salute.

William Adams of the Royal Navy HMS *Wasp*
Within hours, I was no longer sick

SOLDIER SEVEN
18th October 1854 Captain Sir William Peel.
Third son of Prime Minister Peel
Following the June fall of Redan
I was awarded the Victoria Cross
But my arm wouldn't heal
And I knew from being in Kingston
Of the Jamaican woman
Who could brew and cure where others failed
So I called upon her services
Knowing she wouldn't refuse
Be it rank or men
She would solicit to them
The equality of her skills.

He salutes SEACOLE, turns and marches away.

Background music becomes more lively to indicate that the party is now taking hold of the company of guests. It is played in-between each soloist.

CHOIR
We are here in our thousands
To honour Mary Seacole
We are here in our thousands
To honour Mary Seacole
Give a 'rah, give a 'rah
Give a 'rah for Mary Seacole
Give a 'rah, give a 'rah
Give a 'rah for Mary Seacole.

MONSIEUR JULLIEN
I am Monsieur Jullien
Patron of this evening
All things spectacular

Will amaze your eyes
Death defying artistes
Lark-like singing maidens
All the best performers
From around the world.

DIRECTION *The orchestra plays 'The Daring Young Man on the Flying Trapeze'.*

MONSIEUR JULLIEN
Close the gates no more may come
Close the gate no more may come
Hundred and hundreds beg to come in
I am sorry this night is full

CHOIR
We are back, we are back,
We are back in our thousands
We are back, we are back,
We are back in our thousands
Soldiers, Lieutenants,
Sailors and captains
Men of the artillery,
Corporals and their Generals
All have gathered
From near and far
To honour Seacole

MONSIEUR JULLIEN
Gentlemen I beseech to look to your ladies
And cover their eyes if they be weak of heart
For the sights I bring before you
Never before have been seen in these parts
Strongmen who can lift an elephant

A strange woman with a bearded face.
A creature who is half man and monkey
And from darkest Africa a lion and its mate.

DIRECTION *orchestra plays bars from 'Entry of the Gladiators: Thunder and Blazes'.*

MONSIEUR JULLIEN
Close the gates
No more may come
Close the gates
No more may come
Hundred and hundreds beg to come in
I am sorry this night is full

CHOIR
We are back, we are back,
For a third night in our thousands
We are back, we are back,
For a third night in our thousands
We are back, we are back,
To honour Mary Seacole
Give a 'rah for Mary Seacole.

JULLIEN moves to the wings stage right leaning in he pulls a black woman onto the stage. She is dressed in rags, her head is bowed but she pulls against the rope she is tethered to. Her expression is one of madness, the crowd gasps in horror at the sight of her.

MONSIEUR JULLIEN
Over the globe, north, south, west, east
Searching for the best to entertain
Never. I repeat never
Has this act been seen before

She was found primitive
Naked for all to see
A wild untamed creature
And not one word could she speak.

WILD AFRICAN WOMAN

I am far from my home
I am so far from my home
I am in a strange land where people point at me
I am so far from my home
I am far from my home
I am so far from my home
Here no one speaks a language like me
I am so far from my home

I sleep in a cage
Like an animal in a cage
I long to kill those who captured me

She suddenly lunges at JULLIEN. The crowd's gasp is loud and audible one woman is heard to scream. JULLIEN strikes her and she falls to the ground.

WILD AFRICAN WOMAN

I am so far from my home
I will die far from my home
I will die so far from my home
I will never again see my family
I am so far from my home

MONSIEUR JULLIEN

Close the gates no more may come
Close the gate no more may come
Hundred and hundreds beg to come in
I am sorry this night is full

CHOIR

We are back, we are back,
We are back in our thousands
We are back, we are back,
We are back in our thousands
Four nights at Surrey Gardens
Thousands and thousands and thousands and thousands
Pledge their money to the special fund
To honour Mary Seacole

MONSIEUR JULLIEN

I Monsieur Jullien
Have little more to say
The world's best in entertainment
Have all passed this way
Little midgets dancing
Giants wrestling
Gypsies playing fiddle
Magicians with their craft
Great actors reacting battles
But like the end of the war
This night must be the last.

CHOIR

We have come
We have come
to honour Mary Seacole
We have come
We have come
to honour Mary Seacole
Give a 'rah, give a 'rah
For Mary Seacole
The nursing heroine
of the Crimean war
Hip hip hooray

Hip hip Hooray
Mary Seacole
Mary Seacole
Mary Seacole
Mary Seacole

The stage is dimmed. Stage right is the old armchair used by SEACOLE who is standing her back to the audience.

SEACOLE *(turns as. she sings moves to the armchair and sits)*
I remember,
I remember them.
I remember,
I remember them.

On the other side of the stage, propped up in bed is NIGHTINGALE, furiously rearranging her pillows.

DIRECTION *Their duet is as if they are in conversation even though the stage is light to indicate they are in different rooms.*

NIGHTINGALE
Each night ten thousand people
Over four nights
makes forty thousand people
Are they mad?
Is it the Great Exhibition
Or a parody of English society
Bring me paper
Give me paper

I need to write
I need to write
some letters

SEACOLE
I shall write to everyone to thank them
Well not everyone
But I should thank them
And acknowledge their sacrifice
For a simple woman of herbs
Who without their grateful patronage
Would surely meet the destitution
That eagerly awaits at every turn
For my company.

NIGHTINGALE
Do not accompany my words with diffidence
Heed what I say comes from experience
Whilst others idled, I walked in war
Read what I write and know, I know more T
hat hygiene must prevail in the battlefield
That more men die from dirt then those who are killed
And it is sluttish behaviour
that brings the deathly disease of dirt
Pamper if you will to this coloured woman
With her simple cures of herbs
But understand that the words I have written
Are deeply engrained with a nurse's wisdom.
Heed my words.

DIRECTION *The two women are silent for a moment, pausing to think, then turning their attention once again to their writings.*

NIGHTINGALE
One, two three, four,
Turn two, three four
So walked the sentry
Down the corridors of death
Four miles of wounded soldiers
Fighting for their last breath
Legs would lie in the gutter
That ran between their beds
Very few men cried out
Very few men cried.

SEACOLE
Cry my son
Let the tears flow my son
There's nothing like weeping
A man's allowed to cry

NIGHTINGALE
I had my own battles
With the Quarter Master's stores
Supplies they ran out
Or never did reach me
What treachery did send the thieves
What bureaucracy did waste those lives?
That a few pennies more would have kept alive
Just a few pennies more.

The music changes to Ska rhythms.

SEACOLE

Every penny, every penny
I used every penny for stock
And passage to this world of hell
Ev-ery penny, ev-ery penny
They would not send me come
Would not recruit me no
So I took my purse and every penny
Ev-ery penny I needed
Ev-ery penny I needed
To use my skill to heal the men
Who have fallen by the Hussar's gun
Every penny I needed

The music changes tempo back to adagio.

NIGHTINGALE

Every morning I would go to check
What the Purveyor had hidden
For supplies were sold to the highest bidder
For they care not a jot for the fighting soldiers.
So I didn't just nurse them
Half the army I clothed
Uniforms be dammed I saw half-naked men
Bundled from ships to fight wars
And it would only have taken
A few pennies more.

The music changes back to Ska

SEACOLE

Every penny I need-ed
Every penny I need-ed
Like a slave I did toil

This was my life's call
No one to pay me
They didn't want me
See my recommendations
Written by very best gentlemen
Who could stop me?
Who dare try?
Enough of this foolishness
I Mary Seacole
Yellow Woman
Mother of the Soldier
Did come
Did arrive.
Check them
Check I!
And remember

Again the tempo slows.

NIGHTINGALE
Remember that though I lie here defeated
It is only my body that wastes away
Not my mind nor my memory
But will you remember me
Validate for all that I have said
And remember well Florence Nightingale.

The following recording is played.

Nightingale's famous speech in support of the Light Brigade
Relief Fund, recorded on Edison Parafine Wax Cylinder, on
30 July 1890.

London.

Nurses enter as the light on NIGHTINGALE dims to the halo of a light before it blacks out. They walk to the centre of the stage where RUSSELL stands on a podium.

RUSSELL *(spoken)*
Today London celebrate
By the generous donation of soldiers
That enabled the founding of the Nightingale Fund
The opening of St Thomas's Hospital
As a dedicated school for nursing

The NURSES exchange places with RUSSELL on the podium and they place their hands down as though upon a Bible.

NURSES *(spoken)*
I solemnly pledge myself before God and in the presence of this assembly, to pass my life in purity and to practice my profession faithfully. I will abstain from whatever is deleterious and mischievous, and will not take or knowingly administer any harmful drug. I will do all in my power to maintain and elevate the standard of my profession, and will hold in confidence all personal matters committed to my keeping and all family affairs coming to my knowledge in the practice of my calling. With loyalty will I endeavour to aid the physician, in his work, and devote myself to the welfare of those committed to my care.

SCENE SEVEN

RUSSELL dons a black clock and tall hat, he bows his head, takes two steps backwards and, walking in a funeral march, takes a seat at the table. His posture indicates the dejection of his situation.

RUSSELL pushes his typewriter to one side and leans his head in his hands. A younger man appears carrying a decanter and glass, which he waves under RUSSELL's nose. RUSSELL indicates that he might be seated. The young man roots in his pockets, bringing out a pen and paper, as RUSSELL helps himself to the brandy.

YOUNG MAN
You liked her

RUSSELL
I admired her
You had to see how she was
Unnerving in her courage
Caring for all who had fell
And humorous in her giving
And a bloody good cook as well.

YOUNG MAN
How did she manage
After the war was won.
With a rapid evacuation
Did all forget what she'd done?

RUSSELL
She and her business partner
were penniless
The moment they stepped to shore
And in 1856 as bankrupts

they could trade no more
But you forget this woman
And all that she had done
Had walked the path of so many
That something had to be done.

YOUNG MAN
Surrey Gardens were spectacular
I have read your reports
But Jullien's costs were enormous
And the dammed Company
Was secretly insolvent
Before the first performance had begun.

RUSSELL
Two hundred and thirty-three pounds
Nine shillings and eight pennies
Was all that was left from ticket sales?
That quadrupled each evening's capacity.

YOUNG MAN
So Mr Russell was it you
Who championed her again
Rallying the people
with the skill of your pen

RUSSELL
It was not I who caused
Parliament's attention
I confess it was *Punch*'s editorial
That demanded action
From Lord Palmerston
And with Victoria's blessings
The states purse was opened.

And though less then hoped for
Her income was secured.

YOUNG MAN
But I hear she gave not pennies
But in pounds to those in need

RUSSELL
Indeed, she was most benevolent
Especially to orphans and widowers
Who had lost a loved one to war?
And in '58 she did not hesitate
To take
One hundred pounds from her purse.

YOUNG MAN
All of this is admirable
But surely then, Count Gleichen lies
For in his bust of her
Four medals on her breast are designed.

RUSSELL
The French Legion of Honour
The Turkish Order of Mejidie
And the Crimean Medal
And the last one with drink
Fogs my memory.

YOUNG MAN
Was she then perfect

RUSSELL
No far from perfect
To those that knew

She had the temper of a vixen
And a nasty disposition too
At times, she caused a quandary
That though coloured her thoughts were white
For sometimes her attitude to the Turks
Was not a pleasant sight

YOUNG MAN
But you'll miss her

RUSSELL
Yes, I will miss her
As much as everyone will
From Princess Alexandra
Who she befriended
To the most common soldier
She cured.

RUSSELL pulls the typewriter towards him and with obvious reluctance takes up a sheet of paper, inserts it and begins to type. A piano soloist of the opening bars of 'Jamaica Farewell'.

RUSSELL *(spoken)*
May 14th 1881
The sun in London was more dim than usual
Though the day was fine
And no birds could be heard to sing
For sixteen days men who have known battle
Held their breath as apoplexy retained its hold
On the dusky woman we all had come to respect
Then on the 17th day she slipped from all who loved her
To lie in a coma for three days and three nights
Never to gain consciousness again.
What wonderful adventures have the heavens yet to hear

When she opens her store by St Peter
And how many lads both young and old
Who too took their leave before their time
Will once again enjoy her ale and well-cooked broth
And be charmed by Mary Seacole
She is buried far from her place of birth
But what land could hold her
What race claim her
A good catholic to all she knew
In Kensal Rise
She has finally been laid to meet her maker.

SCENE EIGHT

Jamaica.

*RUSSELL stands, the lights reflect the glare of a harsh sun.
RUSSELL removes his jacket, then his tie and undoes his collar
button. He takes a handkerchief out and mops his head and neck
almost feverishly. A Black 'boy' enters carrying a camera, he trips
and RUSSELL admonishes him for his clumsiness. RUSSELL
has now become a World War Two journalist.*

*A BOY enters stage right and as he walks across the stage he
stumbles.*

BOY
Whop mi foot nearly tip mi up
Mi left want to move wid mi right
Mi heart almost stop cos mi tink mi drop
Dis camera that mi hold soh tight

RUSSELL

Good God boy are you stupid
Don't move
Don't flinch
If the likes of you join the army
Hitler's bound to win

RUSSELL grabs the camera, pushes the boy away and busies himself with the apparatus. The BOY watches him, then lifts the cloth to peer underneath.

BOY

Wat yuh do uder der mister White man
Tel mi wat yuh seh
For mi uncle he sails now to Ingland
To fight de British enemi
And he tel mi he will send mi
A picture of de King
And him do it with someting
Dat look just like dis thing

RUSSELL

Good God boy are you stupid don't move
don't flinch
If the likes of you join the army
Hitler's bound to win

Again he pushes the BOY away. The BOY looks back at RUSSELL then goes to sit next to a young GIRL. The GIRL is sobbing.

BOY

Why yuh cry soh
Why yuh cry soh

Why yuh cry soh
Why yuh cry soh
Come look here
Check dis man here
If dis man not a fool then mi lie

GIRL
I cry for mi fadher
Who do sail today
To join the RAF
An' mi uncle
In de merchant navy
Now only mi mudder left
Now dey come cry
To the wimmin too
Qualified nurses
An' those who wish to train
Sayin
Ingland she needs yuh.

*The BOY sings in the same rhythm of the local man Act One Scene
Two who drank too much rum.*

BOY
All dis war is curse for we
Jamaica should be independent
For de English to dis colony
Have only brought lament
What dey brings nuthink?
What deys do nuthink?
What dey leave nuthink?
Gawd save Jamaica and dam de King.
Gawd save Jamaica and dam de King.

GIRL

Sshh! yuh is badd bhoy
Someone shou'd cum lick yuh
Fi dat mouth of yuh
Dos run like fool
Wat yuh don't know
yuh show
Wat yuh don't know
yuh show

The GIRL skips over to the white man who pops his head from under the cloth and without speaking pushes her into a pose.

The BOY watches for a time then wanders away.

RUSSELL

Let me take your picture little urchin
Your image will be a change in my reporting
Now we are recruiting from the Caribbean
You're an inspirational sight.
Do you have a mother, do you know her?
Is she still on the island or has she gone?
To join the call for Nurses
So Miss Nightingale's spirit lives on.
And when you are grown will you join too
Miss Nightingale School could make a nurse of you

GIRL

Miss Nightingale who is dat sar
I never before heard that name

RUSSELL

She is the most famous nurse in the world

GIRL
Noh sar not here sar
But a nurse I will be
But in the name of Mary Seacole
She is a heroine to mi

RUSSELL
Mary Seacole?

GIRL
Yuh not know her
Fancy yuh all clever
An' fine cloths
Sit an' I will tell yuh
How her story goes
No Anansi did tell mi
Wat I sey is de truth
She is heroine of history
And I is proud dat she
Was a Jamaican too

GIRL *(spoken)*
It was a long time ago in Kingston Jamaica
Dat she borne
Mary Jane Grant
Daughter of Mrs Grant
and she husband a white man
who did wear a skirt
and call himself Scottish.
And she wanted to be a nurse
but they would not let her

The orchestra begins to play in a reggae beat as the girl sings:
I am not defeated by rejection

It serves to heighten my determination
I am not defeated by rejection
It serves to heighten my determination
Of this one thing I am sure

THE CHOIR *(joins in to what is now is a chant)*
We are not defeated by rejection
It serves to heighten our determination
we are not defeated by rejection
It serves to heighten our determination

SEACOLE *(walks on singing)*
Of this one thing I am sure
I am not defeated by rejection
It serves to heighten my determination
Then I shall sail by any means
I would walk t'is sorrow I cannot fly
But I will arrive there by and by
I am not defeated by rejection

CHOIR
We are here
To honour Mary Seacole
We are here
To honour Mary Seacole
Give a 'rah, give a 'rah
Give a 'rah for Mary Seacole
Give a 'rah, give a 'rah
Give a 'rah for Mary Seacole.

THE END

PProducer	Larry Coke
Composer	Richard Chew
Librettist	SuAndi

Director	David Edwards
Admin	Jan Ryan
Designer	Janey Gardiner
Education	Judy Hepburn
Lighting	Hartley T. A. Kemp
Choreographer	Jackie Guy
Costume	Rosie Gwilliam
Wardrobe Ass	Lee Croucher
Company SM	Pam Allen
DSM	Annabel Busher
Hair	Sandra Rowe
Photography	Andy Myers and Gemma Mount
Graphic Design	Garry @ Pineapple Publishing
Children's Advisor	Val Schöne and Charles Pindar
Chaperones	Rosie Nixon and Janet O'Connor
Repetiteurs	Jonathan Gale, Julia Richter and Annette Saunders, Pro Musica Chorus x
Secretary	William Ryder,
Music Director	Robert Hamwee

INSTRUMENTAL ENSEMBLE
Steve Morris
Eloise Prouse
Rebecca Chambers
Robin Thompson-Clarke
Charlotte Hooper-Greenhill
Susie Hodder-Williams
Graham Casey
Oliver Preece
Richard Ashton
Tim Gunnel

International Highland Piper: Greg Gordon

I am always amused when I hear a poet give a long explanation for the poem they are about to read, then end the introduction with 'I think the poem speaks for itself!'

However, for me there are times when there is an immediate urge to write (OK inspiration). Normally one write, no edit. These sources should be acknowledged. They are sources which in themselves I hope you, the reader, will find interesting.

---

[1] 'I'm tired of protesting outside' – A line from the script of *Mrs. America* (miniseries), 2020.

[2] An article I read that said no one says 'Motherf****r' like Amiri Baraka.

[3] A John Agard quote.

[4] Grandmother of Adam McKinney a Black, Jewish choreographer with whom I worked in New York. He is presently Artistic Director, Pittsburgh.

[5] Abasindi Cooperative, formed in 1980 in Manchester.

[6] The title song from the 1964 James Bond film of the same name.

[7] From the musical *Sweet Charity*.

[8] *Brookside* set in Liverpool, a Channel 4 soap opera which ran from 1982 until 2003.

[9] Lynette Goddard, Professor of Black Theatre and Performance, read an extract from debbie tucker green's play *Stoning Mary* – I wrote the moments minutes later.

[10] Known for affordable fashion from 1922 and a fixture on UK high streets for decades.

[11] A co-facilitator of a NBAA UK–European project, who shared his father's rejection of him for being gay.

[12] Written for Lemn Sissay

13 Sophia is the eldest daughter of my late childhood friend Yvonne Christian.

14 Written for Dels.

15 In Memory of Shirley Gordon, Manchester Cultural Activist and one of the founders of Abasindi Cooperative.

16 Jamaican poet Elean Thomas (1947–2004), after she shared meeting her mother after years of absence.

17 Part of TV advertising campaign

18 Dr Emma Liggins, a Reader in English Literature at Manchester Metropolitan University, shared how her son loves Sinatra.

19 Branded seating design.

20 British department store 1856–2010.

21 Primary School Greenheys, Manchester, known as 'The League of Nations', due to its pupils' diversity and for having the boy's playground on the roof.

22 After getting lost, I arrived late at a special needs school. A young girl beleaguered me all day, telling me that even she knew where the school was, and she was a 'bit slow'.

23 Heed Sakonfa: Twi language of Ghana, meaning 'go back, look for, and gain wisdom'.

24 'Talking to Stanley on the Telephone' By poet Michael Schmidt.

25 British band of twin brothers from the 1980s and '90s.

26 A permanent wave hairstyle popular during the 1980s and early '1990s.

27 Kirk Washington Jr. 1975–2016.

28 This was a MMU commission for a public art piece that never materialised.

29 National Black Arts Alliance photographic exhibition Once We Were Africans.

30 A pounded meal found in West African cuisine.

31 Relating to their work during Moss Side Riots.

32 George Stubbs, 1724–1806, oil on canvas Manchester City Art Gallery (MCAG).

33 The African American Shakespearean Actor Ira F. Aldridge, 1807–1867.

34 Gurminder Sikand, 1960–2021.

35 After I heard his paper at INIVA Conference, 1994.

36 'Like Fado', by poet Graham Mort.

37 The 1990 Riots (later renamed to HMP Manchester).

38 'A Brief History of Seven Killings', by Marlon James

39 'Like a Blue Mahoe' (Talipariti elatum) is native to the islands of Cuba and Jamaica, where it is the national tree.

40 African-American slang for figures of authority, including police & slave master.

41 Video by John Akomfrah, Bluecoat Liverpool, 2012, based on the life work of Professor Stuart Hall, 1932–2014.

42 President of the USA 2009–17.

43 Nine deaths in the anti-black mass shooting on 17 June 2015 in Charleston, South Carolina.

44 Winnie Mandela was convicted in 1991 of the 1998 kidnapping Stompie Sepe; he died in 1989.

45 English entertainer and television presenter of a seventy-five-year career

46 The burial site of a young slave, on unconsecrated ground in a field near the small village of Sunderland Point, England.

47 Unlicensed late night dance party usually held in houses

ACKNOWLEDGEMENTS

Thanks to John McAuliffe for his editing patience, and to the Carcanet team: my favourite two Mexicans for keeping my spirit going.

I thank the editors of publications in which some of these poems have previously appeared; I ask those of other publication for their forgiveness if I have failed to include them – it has been a very long time.

Catching Hell and Doing Well (Trentham Books, IOE Press)
Out of Bounds (Bloodaxe)
Love Anthology (Shorelines)
Hair (Suitcase)
Reading the Applause (Huddersfield University)
Penguin Book of New Black Writing (Penguin)
Healing Strategies for Women at War (Crocus)
Fire People (Payback Press)
Akwaaba (Pankhurst Press)
100 Black Kisses (Runagate Press)
IC3 (Penguin Books)
PPQ (Poetry Postcards / Peter Taylor)
Africa Refugee (AF Publishing Collective)
Routes and Roots (E.J. Arnold Education Suppliers)
Preston Alternative Poets (Angus Press)
Affirming the Flame (Community Projects Foundation)
Holding Out (Crocus Books)
Black and Priceless (Commonword Books)
Sistahs (Commonword Books)
BlackScribe (BlackScribe / GMVC)
Grass Roots in Verse (Hansib Publishing)
Poetic Licence (Commonword Books)

Mary Seacole libretto, *Hidden Gems, vol. II*, ed. Deirdre Osborne (London: Oberon, 2012).

Some of these poems previously appeared elsewhere:
'The Wig', 'Nando's' and 'I Am, Your Family' were previously published in *Story of M*, Oberon Books, 2017.
'I'm Tired of Protesting Outside' and 'Fou-Fou Youth' were featured in Voices for Freedom (Video).
'The Children' was featured in Everybody Deserves Space, Ruskin's Manchester Now (Video).

Some poems were originally commissioned by different organisations and curators, and I thank:
Manchester Art Gallery; MMU; NBAA Photographic Exhibition 2006 'Once We Were Africans', Manchester Science Museum

Some poems have been anthologized for younger readers, and I wish to thank the editors of:
Rainbow World (Hodder; children's book)
The Works (Macmillan; children's book)
Dear Future – A Time Capsule of Poems (Hodder; children's book anthology)
Specials! (Folens; poetry text book)
Doin Mi Ed In (Macmillan; Anthology)
Unzip Your Lips (Macmillan)
Womens' Talk (Hyndburn Young Women's Group, Lancs. C.C. Youth Service)

Many of the poems have also been recorded, and I thank the producers of:
Seven Sisters (Mongrel Press)
Mother Country (Tak Tak Tak; anthology, 2005)
Soliloquy (Bop Cassettes BIP 601)
Homelands (Bop Cassettes BIP 703 anthology magazines)

For a full list of SuAndi's publications, see the SussedBlackWoman website.
https://mixedmuseum.org.uk/sussedblackwoman/

Book Cover: 'Leaning against Time', recycled paper sculpture by Faith Bebbington. https://faithbebbington.co.uk/

Book Cover image. Joel Fildes. https://tinyurl.com/3ujn3vu9

Photograph of SuAndi © Julian Kronfli. https://juliankronfli.com/

Disclaimer: I hope no one will be offended by what is considered a racist slur, which I have used in some poems. The word is appropriate to the poetic theme.